CANADIAN
SKIN
AND
SCALES

Pat E. Bumstead

Norman H. Worsley

Simply Wild Publications Inc
100 Lake Lucerne Close SE
Calgary, AB T2J 3H8

www.simplywildpub.com

Bumstead, Pat 1952-
    Canadian Skin and Scales

Includes bibliographical references and index.
ISBN 0-9689278-1-5

1. Reptiles—Canada—Juvenile literature. 2. Amphibians—Canada—Juvenile literature.
    I. Worsley, Norman H. 1924-   II. Title

    QL644.2.B85 2003   j597.9'0971   C2003-910829-5

Cover design: Jeremy A.S. Drought, Last Impression Publishing Service

Illustrations by Norman H. Worsley

Printed in Canada

Cover Photographs

Short-horned lizard © Stephen Glendinning
Plains Garter Snake, Painted Turtle, Tiger Salamander, Northern Leopard Frog ©
Brian Wolitski, BMW Wildlife Photography

Attention Schools and Organizations

Quantity discounts are available on bulk purchases of this book for educational purposes. Special books or book excerpts can be created to fit specific needs. For information, please contact Simply Wild Publications, 100 Lake Lucerne Close SE, Calgary, AB T2J 3H8.
Phone 1-877-278-5999 Fax (403)279-3304
www.simplywildpub.com

Foreword

Have you ever been startled by a frog leaping out of the way as you walk through wet grass? Have you ever watched a garter snake hunt at the edge of a pond? Such encounters with wildlife are a window into the workings of the natural world. Frogs and toads, salamanders, snakes, turtles and even lizards may be found in the most unexpected places across this country. Wood Frogs are found well above the Arctic Circle so people living in parts of Yukon, or NWT may see them without travelling too far from home. In the east, Wood Frogs are found as far north as Hudson Bay. From urban backyards and inner city parks to Maritime beaches or BC rainforests amphibians and reptiles are all around but most people rarely see them.

Getting close to amphibians and reptiles takes sharp eyes and ears, the ability to walk up to a pond quietly or sit still for many minutes. It may require searching under logs and rocks, carefully replacing them as found. In the few parts of the country where rattlesnakes are found it also requires some caution. But apart from insects and worms, what other wild animals are there that we can hold in our hands and meet face to face?

Once found we need to treat them respectfully. Frogs, toads and salamanders can be easily injured by rough handling or even killed by absorbing insect repellent or suntan lotion from our hands. Animals moved too far from familiar areas may get lost and perish in unfamiliar surroundings. But with care and respect they will teach us much, and even amateurs can contribute to our scientific knowledge of these animals. For example, we still don't know the full distribution of many species or details of where and when they lay eggs or give birth in different parts of the country.

This information is becoming increasingly important, for as familiar as amphibians and reptiles are to us, they are also the most endangered groups of verte-brates in Canada. More than half of all reptile species and four-tenths of all amphibian species in Canada are listed as federally at risk. Loss of biodiversity (number of species) is a global conservation issue but it is also a local issue. Every one of us can contribute to conservation of amphibians and reptiles: by treating the animals we see gently; by keeping our wetlands and forests clear of litter and pollution; by setting aside habitat (long grass, temporary pools or woody debris) in our yards and gardens; by watching out for them on roads in spring and fall.

This book can be your starting place to discover amphibians and reptiles, what they can teach you and what you can do for them.

Enjoy!

Carolyn Seburn and David Seburn -- authors of "Conservation Priorities for the Amphibians and Reptiles of Canada" published by World Wildlife Fund Canada and the Canadian Amphibian and Reptile Conservation Network (CARCNET).

Amphibians and Reptiles of the World

Class Amphibia		
Caceilians	176 species	6 families
Salamanders and Newts	473 species	10 families
Frogs and Toads	4,750 species	28 families

Class Reptilia		
Turtles and Tortoises	293 species	14 families
Lizards	4,560 species	20 families
Worm Lizards	140 species	4 families
Snakes	2,718 species	18 families
Tuatara	2 species	1 family
Crocodilians	23 species	3 families

Contents

 This symbol in the book indicates a species in trouble in Canada.

Canadian Creatures

CANADIAN CREATURES

Canada is a vast country of nearly 10 million square kilometres. It stretches 4,800 km from the Atlantic to the Pacific, and 4,500 km from its southern border to the northern limit of land on Ellesmere Island in the Arctic.

Within this huge expanse are tremendously diverse life zones– the Arctic tundra, ocean coastlines, prairie grasslands, mountains, and four different types of forest. With the exception of the northern tundra, each of these zones is home to animals that depend on external heat sources to survive.

Animals that require a heat source from outside their body are called *ectothermic*. Once called cold-blooded, this term is no longer used, as it gives the impression they are cold to the touch. The body temperature of amphibians and reptiles is usually not much cooler than that of birds or mammals. They control their temperature by moving from warm places to cooler ones, and back again.

Famous for our harsh and variable climate, it seems astonishing that these animals can survive here. But survive they do, and with some amazing adaptations.

> Unlike humans, these animals do not need to eat on a regular basis to produce body heat and energy. They can go for long periods without eating. This means they can live in remote areas with scarce prey.

Strength in Numbers

OVERWINTERING IN THE NEST—All turtles must come on land to lay their eggs in a nest chamber dug deep in soft soil. The young turtles break their way out of their shell with a temporary egg tooth, and dig their way to the surface. If the temperature on the surface is not warm enough when they hatch, they will spend the winter deep in the protective nest chamber, emerging in the spring.

WORKING AS A GROUP— During the winter, reptiles rely on warm, dry den sites that provide protection from the elements. The temperature in the chosen den never drops below freezing. Snakes are often found in dens, or hibernaculums, numbering several hundred animals. Even species that are enemies during the summer months will spend the winter huddled together. Many species of turtle also **hibernate** in groups.

For many salamander, lizard and snake species, communal nesting sites are the answer. Multiple females will lay their eggs in a particularly choice site, rather than use a less desirable one on their own. This improves the chance of a successful hatching, and is common in areas where good nesting sites are scarce.

Freeze Proof

FREEZE TOLERANT—In the cool **temperate regions**, some species of frog freeze solid during the winter, and can survive temperatures as low as -6°C. To do this, their body increases specialized protein and glucose levels to protect the cells from freezing and drying out. Ice crystals form beneath the skin and throughout the muscles. Up to 60% of their body fluids freeze, blood circulation stops and the heart stops pumping. In the spring, they thaw out and resume normal activities.

HIDING BELOW THE FROST—Many species of amphibian and reptile look to holes in the ground to protect them from freezing. A few species dig their own burrow, but most will use one that has been abandoned by a small mammal. The temperature of the ground below the frost level is warm enough for them to survive the winter.

Aquatic amphibians may spend the winter in water that is too deep or fast flowing to freeze solid. Beneath the ice, there is enough oxygen in the water to keep them alive. Some species of salamander may be seen swimming beneath the frozen surface of their pond. **Tadpoles** and salamander **larvae**, if they don't develop into land-dwelling adults their first season, spend the winter buried in the mud at the pond bottom. Some turtle species also overwinter in the bottom pond sediment.

Darker is Better

BEING DARKER - Dark colours absorb heat from the sun more readily than lighter ones. **Larvae** of most amphibians are dark green, brownish or black. They often swarm together, increasing the size of the mass to attract more heat. Eggs are also laid in large masses so the small dark **embryos** can attract more heat.

This rule also holds true for many of our reptiles. Their tropical cousins are bright and colourful, but ours are various shades of brown. Reptiles living this far from the equator need to receive as much heat as they can from the weaker sun rays.

Using Nature's Supplies

ALGAE GROWING ON EGGS—Frogs and salamanders lay jelly-like masses of eggs. The thick jelly holding the mass together acts as an insulator against the cold. Sometimes these egg masses support the growth of a dark green algae, which provides additional temperature protection, as well as **camouflage**.

RETREATING UNDERGROUND—Winter isn't the only problem season for these animals. Hot, dry conditions can be fatal to amphibians, and many will retreat underground until conditions improve. Using abandoned animal burrows, cavities under tree roots, or shelters in rocks they will hide until it's safe to return to the surface. During long periods of drought, they can go into a kind of dormancy similar to **hibernation**, which is called *aestivation*.

HIBERNATING—With so little to protect their bodies from the elements, reptiles and amphibians use a variety of locations for shelter. Aquatic species may snuggle down into the mud on the bottom of ponds. Turtles can often be found in muskrat or beaver lodges, below the water line. Snakes look for a large, deep rock pile with a warm central area. Salamanders in the moist woodlands survive tucked deep under tree roots, leaf litter, soil and other debris on the forest floor.

Raring to Go

LIVE BORN YOUNG—Many reptile species, instead of laying eggs and leaving them to the elements, retain the eggs inside their bodies and give birth to live young. If the female keeps the eggs inside her body until they hatch, she is better able to regulate their temperature. This is a distinct survival advantage in cooler regions. The warmer the **incubation** temperature, the faster the development of the **embryos** as well.

There is a trade-off for this protective nurturing, as it results in fewer broods. In the tropics, reptiles may reproduce many times a year. Females in the cooler regions who give birth to live young are only able to do so once every year or two. They give birth in the summer, and may be unable to feed enough before **hibernation** to reproduce the following year. Live bearers who live at higher elevations may produce a brood only every two or three years.

 **The following pages contain a list of all amphibian and reptile species found in each province. How many live near you?**

British Columbia (33) Species

Salamanders	Frogs & Toads	Turtles	Lizards	Snakes
Roughskin Newt	Tailed Frog	Painted	Northern Alligator	Rubber Boa
Long-toed	Boreal Chorus Frog		Western Skink	Racer
Northwestern	Pacific Treefrog			Sharptail
Tiger	Bullfrog			Night
Pacific Giant	Spotted Frogs (2)			Gopher
Wandering	Green Frog			Garter Snake (3)
Coeur D'Alene	Leopard Frog			Western Rattler
Ensatina	Red-legged Frog			
Western Redback	Wood Frog			
	Western Toad			
	Gr. Basin Spadefoot			

Alberta (18) Species

Salamanders	Frogs & Toads	Turtles	Lizards	Snakes
Long-toed	Boreal Chorus Frog	Painted	Short-horned	Western Hognose
Tiger	Columbia Spotted			Gopher
	Leopard Frog			Garter Snake (3)
	Wood Frog			Western Rattler
	Canadian Toad			
	Great Plains Toad			
	Western Toad			
	Plains Spadefoot			

Saskatchewan (19) Species

Salamanders	Frogs & Toads	Turtles	Lizards	Snakes
Tiger	Boreal Chorus Frog	Painted	Short-horned	Racer
	Leopard Frog	Snapping		Western Hognose
	Wood Frog			Smooth Green
	Canadian Toad			Gopher
	Great Plains Toad			Red-bellied
	Plains Spadefoot			Garter Snake (3)
				Western Rattler

Manitoba (23) Species

Salamanders	Frogs & Toads	Turtles	Lizards	Snakes
Blue-spotted	Boreal Chorus Frog	Painted	Prairie Skink	Western Hognose
Tiger	Grey Treefrog (2)	Snapping		Smooth Green
Mudpuppy	Spring Peeper			Red-bellied
	Green Frog			Garter Snake (2)
	Mink Frog			
	Leopard Frog			
	Wood Frog			
	American Toad			
	Canadian Toad			
	Great Plains Toad			
	Plains Spadefoot			

Ontario (48) Species

Salamanders	Frogs & Toads	Turtles	Lizards	Snakes
Eastern Newt	Boreal Chorus Frog	Painted	Five-lined Skink	Racer
Blue-spotted	East. Gray Treefrog	Spotted		Ringneck
Jefferson	Nor. Cricket Frog	Wood		Eastern Fox
Smallmouth	Spring Peeper	Box		Black Rat
Spotted	West. Chorus Frog	Blanding's		Eastern Hognose
Four-toed	Bullfrog	Common Map		Milk
Dusky	Green Frog	Musk		Water
Nor. Two-lined	Mink Frog	Snapping		Smooth Green
Redback	Leopard Frog	Spiny Softshell		Queen
Mudpuppy	Pickerel Frog			Brown
	Wood Frog			Red-bellied
	American Toad			Garter Snakes (3)
	Fowler's Toad			Massasauga Rattler

Quebec (35) Species

Salamanders	Frogs & Toads	Turtles	Lizards	Snakes
Eastern Newt	East. Gray Treefrog	Painted	none	Ringneck
Blue-spotted	Spring Peeper	Spotted		Milk
Spotted	West. Chorus Frog	Wood		Water
Four-toed	Bullfrog	Blanding's		Smooth Green
Mountain Dusky	Green Frog	Common Map		Brown
Dusky	Mink Frog	Musk		Red-bellied
Nor. Two-lined	Leopard Frog	Snapping		Common Garter
Redback	Pickerel Frog	Spiny Softshell		
Spring	Wood Frog			
Mudpuppy	American Toad			

Nova Scotia (23) Species

Salamanders	Frogs & Toads	Turtles	Lizards	Snakes
Eastern Newt	Spring Peeper	Painted	none	Ringneck
Blue-spotted	Bullfrog	Wood		Smooth Green
Spotted	Green Frog	Blanding's		Red-bellied
Four-toed	Mink Frog	Snapping		Garter Snake (2)
Nor. Two-lined	Leopard Frog			
Redback	Pickerel Frog			
	Wood Frog			
	American Toad			

Prince Edward Island (12 Species)

Salamanders	Frogs & Toads	Turtles	Lizards	Snakes
Eastern Newt	Spring Peeper	none	none	Smooth Green
Blue-spotted	Green Frog			Red-bellied
Spotted	Leopard Frog			Common Garter
Redback	Wood Frog			
	American Toad			

New Brunswick (23 Species)

Salamanders	Frogs & Toads	Turtles	Lizards	Snakes
Eastern Newt	East. Gray Treefrog	Painted	none	Ringneck
Blue-spotted	Spring Peeper	Wood		Smooth Green
Spotted	Bullfrog	Snapping		Red-bellied
Four-toed	Green Frog			Common Garter
Dusky	Mink Frog			
Nor. Two-lined	Leopard Frog			
Redback	Pickerel Frog			
	Wood Frog			
	American Toad			

Newfoundland (7 Species)

Salamanders	Frogs & Toads	Turtles	Lizards	Snakes
Blue-spotted	Green Frog	none	none	none
Nor. Two-lined	Mink Frog			
	Leopard Frog			
	Wood Frog			
	American Toad			

Yukon (4 Species)

Salamanders	Frogs & Toads	Turtles	Lizards	Snakes
none	Boreal Chorus Frog	none	none	none
	Columbia Spotted			
	Wood Frog			
	Western Toad			

Northwest Territories (6 Species)

Salamanders	Frogs & Toads	Turtles	Lizards	Snakes
none	Boreal Chorus Frog	none	none	Common Garter
	Leopard Frog			
	Wood Frog			
	Canadian Toad			
	Western Toad			

Nunavit (2 Species)

Salamanders	Frogs & Toads	Turtles	Lizards	Snakes
none	Wood Frog	none	none	none
	American Toad			

Most of the amphibians and reptiles found in Canada have bigger ranges in the USA, and none are exclusively Canadian. While most are located in the southern portion of the country, a few hardy species live as far north as the tree line.

Amphibians

AMPHIBIANS

These animals must have water. It keeps their skin moist, and is essential for the development of their eggs and **larvae**. They live in, or near, freshwater ponds, marshes and rivers on every continent except Antarctica. They are divided into three **Orders**: caecilians, which are not found in Canada; newts and salamanders; and frogs and toads.

The word amphibian comes from two Greek words *amphi* and *bios* that mean 'double life'. They are the only animals that go through a complete change of body form, called **metamorphosis**. The young **larvae** live in water, breathe through **gills** and eat plants. As they grow, they develop legs and lungs, change their diet to animal matter and live on land.

The Outside Story

Amphibians have thin skin like the linings of our lungs, with no fur, hair, scales or feathers. This naked skin acts as a respiratory surface through which they take in oxygen and dispel carbon dioxide. Many species also breathe through **gills**, lungs or mouth linings.

Like their reptile cousins, amphibians are always growing and have to keep shedding the outer layer of their skin. They shed their skin in small patches. These patches are seldom found, as the animal usually eats them. How often they shed depends on how much they eat and how fast they grow.

Many produce a **toxic** chemical in their skin. They cannot bite or sting with it, and the poison only works if a predator tries to eat them.

Colours Count

Amphibians come in a huge variety of colours and patterns. Many species are darker on top but brightly coloured underneath. When they move, these **flash colours** are thought to startle a predator into hesitating, allowing them to escape. Some have bright colours to indicate they are poisonous.

Metamorphosis of the Frog

Tadpole hatches

External gills appear

Gills covered in skin

Hind feet appear

Front feet appear

Tail is absorbed

Some can change colour depending on the surrounding air temperature and humidity. Warm dry conditions mean they are paler, and they darken in cool, damp areas. They do this by controlling the flow of black **pigment** to their skin. This lets them blend into their surroundings, or control how the skin absorbs heat.

New Generations

Most frogs and toads lay jelly-like egg masses in the water, and reproduce with a process called external **fertilization**. The male climbs on the back of the female as she lays her eggs. He wraps his arms around her body just behind her front legs, in a position called *amplexus*. In this position, he is able to fertilize the eggs as they are laid. The Tailed Frog is the exception to this practice, as they live in fast flowing streams that carry the **sperm** away from the eggs, so **fertilization** must be internal.

Salamanders have a different method of reproducing. The male places a packet of **sperm** called a *spermataphore* on the ground. Then he guides the female over top of it, and she picks it up in her reproductive tract, or *cloaca*. The eggs are then fertilized as they are laid. Some salamanders lay soft shelled eggs in damp places on land, and these **larvae** complete their development inside the egg.

Protecting Themselves

Although they may seem defenceless, these animals are masters at blending into their surroundings. Remaining motionless, hiding, and fleeing are also used to escape. Some salamanders have aggressive displays to warn off intruders, and some break off the tip of their tail to distract predators. Muscle contractions make the tip twitch, distracting the predator so the animal can escape.

> The world's most dangerous animal is the mosquito. Excluding wars and accidents, these animals have been responsible for 50 percent of all human deaths since the Stone Age. Amphibians help control mosquito populations.

Dinner is Served

Amphibians are excellent pest controllers, and consume large quantities of insects, including mosquitoes and their **larvae**, slugs, earthworms and other small creatures. Larger species may also consume mice, shrews, small fish and other amphibians. They hunt by sight, actively seeking their prey or sitting still until it comes near enough to be captured. Food is swallowed whole because they do not have cutting or crushing teeth.

Tadpoles, amphibian **larvae** and adults are also a very important food source for fish, birds, mammals, reptiles and other amphibians. This energy source allows a whole host of creatures to live and reproduce their own young.

About the Future

A number of years ago, scientists became alarmed at the increasing number of deformities in amphibians, such as extra legs or heads. Because of their **porous** skin, amphibians are extremely sensitive to any changes in the environment. Some scientists think the increased number of deformities is due to the contamination of our air by pesticides, acid rain, pollution and increased UV radiation caused by global warming. Amphibian populations around the world have been dropping rapidly since the 1970's, and the trend continues.

The frog was a symbol of female fertility in ancient Egypt, and women often wore amulets depicting these animals.

*

Many cultures associate frogs with rain; it is generally thought that if you harm a frog a heavy rain will follow; American Indians and Australian Aborigines considered the croaking of frogs as a sign rain was coming.

*

European violinists of the 18th and 19th century rubbed their hands across the backs of toads to halt perspiration.

*

In Burmese and Indo-Chinese legend, a frog caused the eclipse by swallowing the moon.

*

The Egyptian hieroglyph for tadpole also stands for the number 100,000.

*

In Japan, frogs are considered good luck.

*

Toads were once associated with witchcraft, and there are records of them being tried, convicted and burned at the stake.

*

Embalmed frogs have been found inside human mummies in the Temple of Thebes.

Salamanders and Newts

SALAMANDERS AND NEWTS

These are among the least familiar animals to most people, and may be confused with lizards because of their similar body shape. Salamanders are secretive, harmless creatures with no scales or claws. Active mainly at night, they live in damp areas under logs or rocks, and make few sounds. One estimate has been made that the total number of woodland salamanders in eastern North America could be higher than that of mammals and birds put together.

The name newt is applied to the partly **aquatic** members of this family. Salamander is the general term for all the others. The word salamander comes from the Greek word for 'fire-lizard'. In ancient times, these animals were credited with the ability to endure fire. When logs where they had taken cover were thrown on the fire, the animals made a quick dash to escape, thus people associated them with fire, and asbestos, a fireproof material, was once called 'salamander's wool'.

Habitat

This varied **Order** includes some that spend all their time in the water, some that spend all their time on land, and some that divide their time between the two areas. There is no typical lifestyle, but all are **carnivorous** in all life stages.

Ideal habitat for these animals is damp woodlands with thick **under story** vegetation, and an abundance of water in the form of ponds, lakes, slow moving streams or swamps with thick submerged vegetation. They make use of temporary pools, stream backwaters and other water bodies with no fish.

Features

Elongated bodies and tails distinguish all the members of this **Order**. With four limbs of nearly equal size, they walk instead of hop, and actively seek prey. Most species have four digits on the front limbs and five on the back. Heads are narrow, and their eyes and mouth are small. They have two nostrils, eyes with moveable eyelids and fine teeth. With no external ears they cannot hear airborne sounds, but do pick up ground vibrations.

Flexible skin is only one method of breathing for these animals: **larvae** have **gills**, some adults have lungs, some have lungs as well as **gills**, and some species breathe through their mouth lining.

> Many species can be identified by the number of skin folds along their sides, known as **costal grooves**. These vertical grooves indicate the position of the ribs, and the number of grooves varies from species to species.

Larvae of some pond dwelling species may develop small projections on the sides of their head. These balancers help them keep their balance until limbs develop, and may prevent them from sinking into the bottom sediment.

Family Life

Some salamanders lay their eggs in humid cavities on land. These young complete their larval stage inside the large-yoked egg, and either parent may guard them until they hatch as miniature versions of the adults. Most species, however, attach their eggs to underwater vegetation. These **larvae** spend a long period of time in the water before changing into sexually mature adults. Some species never change to adults, but remain and breed in the larval form, which is known as a **neotenic** state.

During breeding season, male Crested Newts of Europe undergo a striking transformation. They acquire brightly coloured dots and stripes, and grow a jagged crest along their back, making them look like tiny dinosaurs.

Stupendous Salamanders !

The largest North American salamander is the Hellbender of the southern USA, which reaches 70 cm.

▼

The body of the California Newt contains a nerve poison so powerful that a tiny drop can kill several thousand mice.

▼

The world's smallest salamander is the Mexican Lungless, which measures just 2.5 cm from nose to tail tip.

▼

The Alpine Newt has a gestation period of 38 months – longer even than that of the elephant. Their young are **cannibalistic** before birth, as most of the eggs carried in the female are eaten by the first developing **embryos**.

▼

The Chinese Giant Salamander averages a metre in length and weighs up to 30 kg. Considered a delicacy, they are often caught with rod and line, and are now endangered.

▼

The Peaks-Of-Otter Salamander is thought to have one of the most limited range of any—they live only along a 19 km stretch in the mountains of Virginia, USA.

▼

The Sharp-ribbed Salamander has ribs that push against and sometimes through the skin. They are so sharp they can draw blood.

▼

Japanese Giant Salamanders have been documented to live 55 years.

▼

Siberian Salamanders, found across Russia, can withstand winter temperatures of −56°C.

▼

The Chinese Spiny Newt has long, sharp, pointed ribs. If bitten, the ribs push out through poison glands in the skin.

▲

Newt Family
Salamandridae

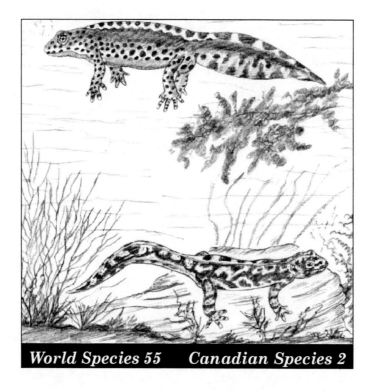

World Species 55   Canadian Species 2

Family Range

This family is mainly European and Asian in its distribution, and newts are found in Europe, Asia, the Middle East, northwest Africa and North America.

Characteristics

Members of this family are extremely poisonous in all life stages, even their eggs. Newts have the most potent skin glands in this family, but their rough-textured skin is not as slippery as salamanders. They do not have any **costal grooves** along the sides. Adults of the **aquatic** species have well developed tail fins. During breeding season, males develop courtship crests along the back and tail.

Reproduction

Reproductive methods differ in the eastern and western species. The eastern animals lay their eggs in water, change to temporary land dwellers called *efts*, then transform again to permanent water-dwelling adults. Sometimes they skip the eft stage and live only in the water. In the western species, eggs are laid in the water and the **larvae** transform directly into land dwelling adults.

Eastern Newt Triton vert
Notophtalmus viridescens

Known for their many life stages, these animals start life in the water as **larvae***, and remain in this state four to six months. They then change into land dwelling 'efts', and remain in this form one to seven years before changing to* **aquatic** *adults.*

Size 5-14 cm

Colour
Brownish or reddish orange; black circled red spots

Reproduction
Up to 400 eggs hatch in 3-8 weeks. Adults appear their first summer.

Where do they live?

➤ Vegetated ponds, marshes, lakes
➤ Ontario to the Maritimes, south to Florida

Did You Know...

◈ Also called Red-spotted or Central Newt
◈ Bright red or orange colours of the eft serve as a warning they are **toxic**
◈ May be seen **foraging** in broad daylight after heavy rains
◈ Adults vary in colour depending on their size and gender
◈ Can be found in water no deeper than one metre; usually seen when they surface to take a gulp of air
◈ Active during the winter; can sometimes be seen under the ice
◈ Capable of locating their breeding pond through true navigation; known to detect the Earth's magnetic field, and may use this as a directional guide
◈ Average eft home range is 270 square metres
◈ Female may store **sperm** up to ten months before laying her eggs
◈ A hungry eft can consume 2,000 insects
◈ Very fond of frog eggs; a rapid temperature drop can trap them in the jelly-like mass where they may freeze
◈ Known lifespan up to fifteen years

Roughskin Newt Triton rugueux
Taricha granulose

One of the most **toxic** *newts in North America, these animals have a defensive posture of lifting the head, turning the tail straight up over the body and extending their limbs. This shows their bright underside, which warns would-be predators they are poisonous.*

Size 5-14 cm

Colours
Brown to black above,
yellow or orange belly

Reproduction
Few dozen eggs hatch in 5-10 weeks. Adults appear their first summer.

Where do they live?

➢ Vegetated ponds, marshes, lakes
➢ Alaska, British Columbia, south to California

Did You Know...

◈ Have rough, warty skin except during breeding season when the males develop a smooth, slimy skin

◈ Skin of both sexes becomes lighter in the breeding season

◈ May be seen hunting on land during humid autumn days

◈ On Vancouver Island, the males may be permanently **aquatic** and only the females return to land after breeding; on the mainland, both sexes leave the water after breeding to **hibernate** on land

◈ Prefer cold, permanent streams; may be found under debris, logs or underground during cold or dry weather

◈ Garter snakes have evolved a resistance to their poison, and are one of their main predators

◈ Have caused illness and death of people who have eaten them, and should not be handled with bare hands

◈ Known lifespan up to three years

Mole Salamander Family
Ambystomatidae

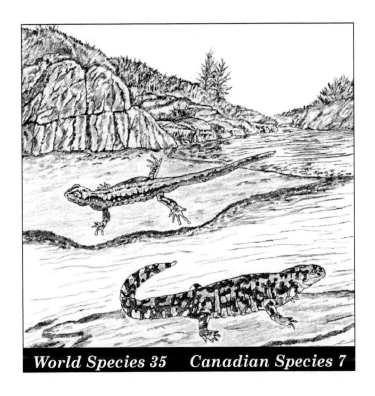

World Species 35   Canadian Species 7

Family Range

This family is found only in North America, and species are widely distributed across the entire continent.

Characteristics

Distinguished by chunky bodies and limbs, they have short, blunt heads and small eyes. As one would expect from their family name, these small animals are known for their secretive underground lifestyle. Adults often remain hidden during the day under rotting logs, leaf litter or stones, and make use of animal burrows for shelter.

Reproduction

These land-dwelling animals **migrate** to breeding ponds in the spring, and clumps of clear, floating eggs are often visible in the clear water. **Larvae** develop in the water, and may change to adults that spend their lives on the land. Some do not change, but become breeding adults and remain in the larval form throughout their lives.

Blue-spotted Salamander Salamandre à pointes bleus
Ambystoma laterale

*When threatened, these animals that seem to lack defences lift their tail up over their body. Glands located on the underside of the tail secret a sticky, **toxic** liquid, and predators that pick them up in their mouth soon drop them and retreat.*

Size 7-14 cm

Colour
Gray to bluish black;
light blue or white flecks

Reproduction
Up to 400 eggs hatch in 3-4 weeks. Adults appear their first summer

Where do they live?

➤ Shallow ponds, bogs, ditches
➤ Manitoba to the Maritimes, south to New Jersey

Did You Know...

◆ Found further north than any other Canadian salamander, up to James Bay, Ontario
◆ Tail is 40% of body length
◆ Smallest member of the Mole Salamander family
◆ **Nocturnal** feeders
◆ Males are smaller than females, but have longer tails
◆ Usually live underground, under rocks or in fallen logs
◆ In captivity, they can survive on one worm a week
◆ Consume great quantities of mosquitoes and their **larvae**
◆ Arrive at breeding ponds in great numbers during spring rains
◆ Males often put their **sperm** packet on top of those deposited by other males
◆ High risk of road mortality in spring breeding **migration**
◆ Known lifespan up to two years

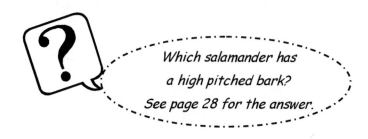

Which salamander has a high pitched bark?

See page 28 for the answer.

Jefferson Salamander Salamandre de Jefferson
Ambystoma jeffersonianum

The tail of these salamanders is vital to their defence, with poison skin glands located at its upper base. If threatened, they raise their tail and lash it around. They may also form a protective coil, tucking their head underneath their tail.

Size 10-21 cm

Colour
Brown, black or gray;
small bluish or whitish flecks

Reproduction
Ten or more masses of about
20 eggs hatch in 4-6 weeks.
Adults appear their first summer.

Where do they live?

➤ Swamps and ponds
➤ Southern Ontario, south to Virginia

Did You Know...

◈ Look exactly like Blue-spotted Salamanders
◈ Can live through near freezing temperatures
◈ Slender animals with long snouts and toes
◈ Tail is almost as long as the body, and can be shed at will
◈ Normal **metamorphosis** occurs in two to three months; if temporary breeding ponds dry up, it will occur sooner
◈ Adults are completely **terrestrial**, often living in abandoned mammal burrows
◈ Used for medical research on re-growth of tissue and limbs
◈ **Migrate** from overwintering site to breeding ponds in spring
◈ Predators include owls, snakes, skunks and raccoons

Threatened

**Loss of habitat
Urban development
Road mortality**

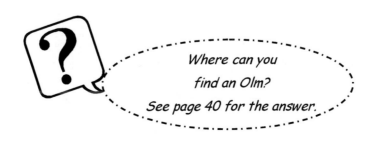

Where can you find an Olm?
See page 40 for the answer.

Long-toed Salamander Salamandre à longs doigts

Ambystoma macrodactylum

Male Long-toed Salamanders arrive at their breeding ponds before the females in late winter, when there is still snow on the ground and ice on the water. Breeding sites are often shared with the Northwestern and other salamander species.

Size 10-17 cm

Colour
Dark brown or black;
yellow or tan back stripe

Reproduction
85-400 eggs hatch and transform
in one season, or overwinter
and transform the next summer.

Where do they live?

➢ Ponds, lakes, slow streams
➢ Alaska, British Columbia, south western Alberta, south to California

Did You Know...

◈ The only Mole Salamander in western Canada with a striped back
◈ Back stripe is sometimes broken up into large blotches
◈ Population in Alberta is restricted to the foothills
◈ Tail is up to half their body length
◈ Retreat underground during hot, dry or freezing weather
◈ Found from sea level to 2,700 metres
◈ Egg masses do not support helpful algae growth, unlike those of the Northwestern Salamander
◈ Eaten by garter snakes and Bullfrogs
◈ Also found on Vancouver Island, BC

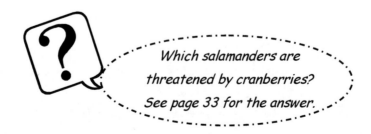

Which salamanders are threatened by cranberries? See page 33 for the answer.

Northwestern Salamander Salamandre foncée
Ambystoma gracile

Cold-tolerant salamanders, these animals can be found up to 3,050 metres. Adults at lower elevations reproduce every year. Those in higher areas, where they reach sexual maturity in the larval stage, breed every other year.

Size 14-22 cm

Colour
Brown, gray or black;
tan belly

Reproduction
Up to 300 eggs hatch in 2-4 weeks. Adults appear within 1-2 years.

Where do they live?

➢ Ponds, lakes, slow streams
➢ Alaska, British Columbia, south to California

Did You Know...

◆ Also known as Brown Salamanders
◆ Secrete a sticky, white substance from glands on the head, body and tail which is mildly irritating to human skin
◆ Make a series of ticking sounds as a warning
◆ If **metamorphosis** to the adult form occurs, it usually takes two years
◆ Defence posture is to raise themselves up, lower the head and lean towards the intruder while lashing their tail
◆ Eggs support the growth of algae, helpful to their development
◆ Secretive and rarely seen, little is known of their life history
◆ Also found on Vancouver Island, BC
◆ Populations at higher levels do not transform to adults, but remain **neotenic**
◆ Known lifespan up to ten years

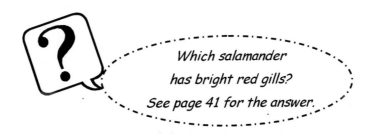

Which salamander has bright red gills? See page 41 for the answer.

Smallmouth Salamander Salamandre à nez court
Ambystoma texanum

These animals are named for their small heads and blunt, short snouts. The head appears swollen behind the eyes. Males are smaller than females, and their tail is more compressed from the side. Their dark colours help hide them in the forest.

Size 10-17 cm

Colour
Dark brown or black; gray or tan blotched markings

Reproduction
Up to 700 eggs hatch in 3-8 weeks. Adults appear their first summer.

Where do they live?

➢ Flooded ditches, ponds, streams
➢ South western Ontario, south to the Gulf Coast

Did You Know...

◆ Adults spend most of their time in burrows, which may be self dug
◆ Need to live in areas with damp debris or loose soil
◆ Seldom enter the water except to breed
◆ Often live in abandoned crayfish burrows
◆ Have a defence posture of raising and whipping their tail around, and tucking their head underneath
◆ Share breeding ponds with Spotted and other salamanders
◆ Breed as soon as ponds are free of ice in early spring
◆ Eggs are laid individually, not in one big mass
◆ Common throughout much of their range in the USA
◆ Eat slugs and worms

Special Concern

Loss of habitat Decreasing water levels

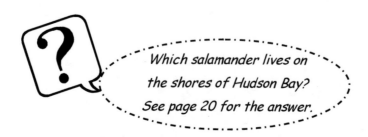

Which salamander lives on the shores of Hudson Bay? See page 20 for the answer.

Spotted Salamander Salamandre maculée
Ambystoma maculatum

These animals remain below ground much of the year. They do not dig burrows, but use those of other animals or cavities under rocks or tree roots. An entire population may live their lives in a small 5-10 hectare area around their breeding pond.

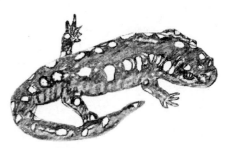

Size 11-24 cm

Colour
Black, dark brown or gray; orange or yellow spots

Reproduction
Up to 300 eggs hatch in 4-8 weeks. Adults appear their first summer.

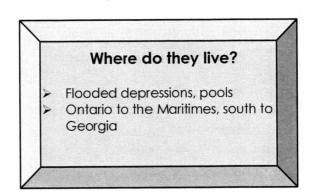

Where do they live?

➤ Flooded depressions, pools
➤ Ontario to the Maritimes, south to Georgia

Did You Know...

◆ Also called Yellow-spotted Salamander
◆ Unspotted individuals occur but are rare; an albino-like form is creamy white with yellow spots
◆ Adults are thought to defend their **territory** with scent marking
◆ **Courtship** includes swimming in groups and rubbing each other with their noses
◆ May **migrate** up to one half a kilometre to and from their breeding sites
◆ Breeding in spring is triggered by early rains
◆ Eggs are laid individually, not in one large mass
◆ Developing egg masses turn green from growths of algae; these eggs hatch earlier and have better survival rates
◆ Acid rain has made water in some areas so acidic that eggs cannot develop
◆ Known lifespan up to twenty five years

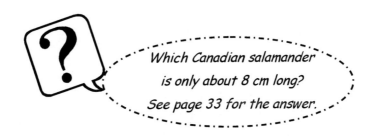

Which Canadian salamander is only about 8 cm long?
See page 33 for the answer.

Tiger Salamander Salamandre tigrée
Ambystoma tigrinum

These salamanders live in almost every habitat. Their adaptability and large range is likely due to the fact they are able to dig their own burrows, and live underground most of the year. This allows them to escape the surface temperature extremes.

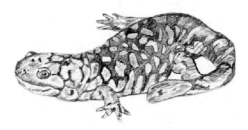

Size 15–30 cm

Colour
Dark or light background
with large bars or blotches

Reproduction
Up to 1000 eggs. **Larvae** do
not always transform to adults,
but may remain in a **neotenic** state.

Where do they live?

➤ Temporary pools, ponds, streams
➤ South western BC, Alberta, Saskatchewan, Manitoba, south to Mexico

Did You Know...

◈ Greatest range of any North American salamander, living in grasslands, mountain forests and damp meadows

◈ World's largest land dwelling salamander

◈ Eat large numbers of earthworms, large insects, snails, small mice and amphibians

◈ Where breeding ponds may dry up, individuals become sexually mature and reproduce in the larval state

◈ Have been found 60 centimetres below the surface

◈ Large females may produce up to 5,000 eggs each year – the largest clutch for any salamander in the world

◈ Breeding is prompted by heavy rains; will make use of man-made water bodies such as canals and dugouts

◈ Threatened by exposure to agricultural chemicals and the use of their **larvae** as fish bait

◈ Thousands killed on the roads as they **migrate** to and from breeding ponds

◈ Lifespan up to twenty-five years

Pacific Mole Salamander Family

Discamptodontidae

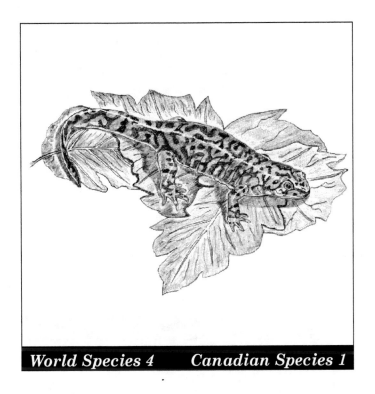

World Species 4   Canadian Species 1

Family Range

This small family may sometimes be called the Pacific Giant Salamander family. They are found only along the western coast of North America, and are placed in a separate family due to their size.

Characteristics

Capable diggers and climbers, these animals have hardened toes for these purposes. They frequently dig to find food or to hide in protective cover. Living in or near mountain streams, they have reduced lungs, which prevent them from being too buoyant and swept away in the current.

Reproduction

White, large-yoked eggs are laid in hidden nest sites on land and guarded by the female until they hatch. **Larvae** feed off the yolk sack for two to three months after hatching, and remain in the nest during this period.

Pacific Giant Salamander Grand salamandre
Dicamptodon tenebrosus

Females of this species guard their eggs in a nest chamber under logs or rocks until they hatch. During this time they eat little or nothing themselves. Because of this long guarding period, these salamanders breed only every other year.

Size 17-30 cm

Colour
Brown, black or purplish;
light marbled patterns

Reproduction
Up to 200 eggs hatch in 25-30 weeks, transform in 1-2 years or remain in **neotenic** state.

Where do they live?

➤ Rivers, clear mountain lakes
➤ South western British Columbia, south to California

Did You Know...

◆ Tail is 40% of body length, and used as an aid in swimming
◆ One of the few salamanders that make any noise; known to emit a high-pitched yelp, bark, scream or rattling sound
◆ Have been seen up to three metres high in trees or shrubs
◆ Known to be aggressive; will bite, thrash tail and use glands on the top of the tail to secrete foul tasting chemicals
◆ Hungry **larvae** eat smaller ones; adults eat mice, shrews and small garter snakes
◆ Young stay in the nest chamber for a few months before moving to water
◆ Sold as pets in the USA
◆ Eaten by garter snakes, weasels, river otters
◆ Known lifespan up to sixteen years

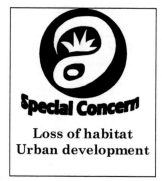

Special Concern

**Loss of habitat
Urban development**

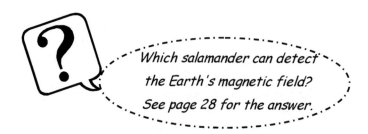

Which salamander can detect the Earth's magnetic field?
See page 28 for the answer.

Lungless Salamander Family
Plethodontidae

World Species 266   Canadian Species 10

Family Range

This is the largest salamander family. They live in North, Central and South America with two species in Europe. They are the only salamanders that live in the tropics.

Characteristics

All members of this family are lungless, and breathe through the skin and the roof of their mouth. They must live in damp habitats, as their skin has to be moist at all times so the blood beneath can take up oxygen. They have grooves running from their nostril to their lip, which carry odours from the ground to their nose. They produce a sticky slime if handled.

Reproduction

Some species defend an area where they feed and mate. Their **courtship** ritual includes rubbing and prodding each other with their noses. Most members of this family lay their eggs on land in underground cavities or rotting logs. Hatchlings of these species are fully formed miniature versions of the adults, and do not go through an **aquatic** larval stage. Others lay their eggs on land, but their **larvae** wriggle their way to water where they complete their development into land-dwelling adults.

Couer D'Alene Salamander _Salamandre de Coeur d'Alene_
Plethodon idahoensis

Some authorities list this salamander and the Washington subspecies of Van Dyke's Salamander as the same species. Whether they are separate or the same, they occupy a very small range, and are found only in small, isolated populations.

Size 6-12 cm

Colour
Black, tan, reddish, with yellow or red stripe on the back

Reproduction
4-12 eggs laid on land.
No **aquatic** larval stage.

Where do they live?

➤ Humid coastal forest
➤ South eastern British Columbia, south to Montana

Did You Know...

◆ Tongue is attached at the front of the mouth
◆ Back stripe may be absent on some individuals
◆ Habits poorly known
◆ Most **aquatic** woodland salamander, living in moist areas near running water
◆ Readily take to fast moving water if disturbed
◆ Eat insects and their larvae that live in water
◆ Female can store **sperm** up to nine months before laying her eggs
◆ Thought the female guards her eggs until they hatch
◆ Sexual maturity reached in three to four years
◆ Males mate every year, but females every other year
◆ First discovered in Canada just over a decade ago

Special Concern

Habitat alteration such as logging Isolated population

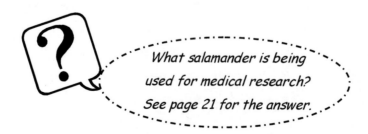

What salamander is being used for medical research? See page 21 for the answer.

Dusky Salamander Salamandre sombre
Desmognathus fuscus

*While the eggs of this species are laid on land, the young are **aquatic**. They only stay in their moist hatching site for a short period before wriggling to water. When their development to adults is complete, they return to a **terrestrial** life.*

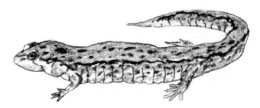

Size 6-14 cm

Colour
Gray, tan or brown, may
have mottled markings

Reproduction
Up to 36 eggs laid on land hatch in
6-13 weeks. **Larvae** turn into
adults in 6-12 months.

Where do they live?

➢ Spring fed creeks
➢ Southern Ontario, Quebec, New
Brunswick, south to Louisiana

Did You Know...

◆ Colour patterns of the adults change as they age; juveniles have orange or red blotches that disappear as they grow

◆ Hind legs are longer and stouter than the front ones

◆ Open their mouth by moving the upper jaw up, not the immovable lower jaw down

◆ Tail is compressed from the side, and has a knife-like edge on top

◆ Small groups of adults and juveniles may be found together

◆ Widespread in the mountain regions of eastern North America; limited to one site in Ontario between Lakes Erie and Ontario

◆ Small home range is about three square metres

◆ Female guards the eggs until they hatch

◆ Known lifespan up to four years

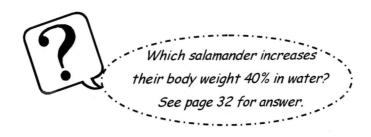

Which salamander increases their body weight 40% in water? See page 32 for answer.

Ensatina Salamandre variable
Ensatina eschscholtzii

If threatened, Ensatinas assume a sway-backed stance and whip their tail around. The tail drips a **toxic**, *milky secretion directed toward the enemy. They are the only Canadian salamander to spray chemicals, and can reach a distance of two metres.*

Size 7-15 cm

Colour
Brown, black or reddish, may have bars, blotches or lighter flecks

Reproduction
5-16 eggs hatch in 4-5 months. No **aquatic** larval stage.

Where do they live?
➤ Humid coastal forest
➤ South western British Columbia, south to Baja

Did You Know...

◇ Also called Oregon Salamander
◇ Found in a variety of colour patterns; dark background may be covered with cream, yellow or orange spots, blotches or marbling
◇ Live up to 3,000 metres
◇ Sexes can be told apart by the length of their tail
◇ May produce a hissing sound when disturbed
◇ Most active spring and fall, when the ground is damp
◇ Retreat into caves, mammal burrows or other crevices during cold or dry conditions, or to **hibernate**
◇ Come out during rains to replenish the water in their body; dry adults can increase their weight 40% when placed in water
◇ Males defend a year round **territory** of 6-40 metres
◇ Eggs are laid in grape-like clusters, and guarded by female until they hatch
◇ Also found on Vancouver Island, BC
◇ Known lifespan up to five years

Four-toed Salamander Salamandre à quatre doigts
Hemidactylium scutatum

*This species has a very specialized habitat require-
ment of boggy areas in hardwood forest, as they lay
their eggs in moss or at moss-laden bases of trees.
Much of this original habitat has been developed,
and there are many small, isolated populations.*

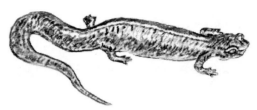

Size 5-10 cm

Colour
Reddish brown, gray or black, white
belly with black spots

Reproduction
20-80 eggs hatch in 6-8 weeks.
Larvae wriggle to water to complete
development to adults.

Where do they live?

➤ Vegetated streams, bogs
➤ Southern Ontario, south western
Quebec, Maritimes, south to Gulf
Coast

Did You Know...

◈ Canada's smallest salamander
◈ Have only four toes on hind feet instead of the usual five of most salamanders
◈ Able to release their tail if threatened and re-grow it; new one is smaller and lighter
in colour
◈ **Hibernate** in groups
◈ In low elevations they stay close to water; at higher altitudes they prefer the forest
floor
◈ Female lays on her back to lay eggs
◈ Eggs are laid on land, **larvae** live in the water and then change into **terrestrial**
adults
◈ Threatened by the conversion of bogs into cranberry producing areas
◈ Known lifespan up to eight years

Mountain Dusky Salamander Salamandre somber des
Desmognathus orcophaeus

Ideal habitat for these salamanders is cool, spring fed, rocky creeks in mountain areas. They inhabit wooded uplands up to 1,900 metres. Those in the lower elevations stay close to water, while those at higher ones favour the cool, moist forest floor.

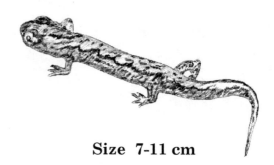

Size 7-11 cm

Colour
Reddish brown, yellow, orange or green, with brown back stripe

Reproduction
24-36 eggs laid on land. **Larvae** wriggle to water to change into adults in 2-8 months.

Where do they live?

➢ Springs, streams, seepage areas
➢ Quebec, south to Alabama

Did You Know...

◈ Climb trees and shrubs at night while looking for food
◈ Ambush prey instead of actively pursuing it
◈ Whole populations may gather together during the winter where the ground is saturated
◈ Females use the same nest site each year, and guard the eggs
◈ Home range is less than one square metre
◈ **Hibernate** in groups
◈ First discovered in Canada in the 1980's
◈ Illegal to keep them as pets in Quebec
◈ Threats include changes to the water table by pumping it to golf courses
◈ Known lifespan up to 15 years

Special Concern

**Loss of habitat
Urban development
Low water table**

?

Which salamander species lays poison eggs?

See page 18 for the answer.

Northern Two-lined Salamander Salamandre à deux lignes
Eurycea bislineata

While these salamanders are thought to be numerous in some areas, much of their life history is unknown. It is thought that in some populations, they do not transform into terrestrial adults, but may reproduce in the larval neotenic state.

Size 6-12 cm

Colour
Yellow, brown or greenish, two dark lines down the back

Reproduction
Up to 100 eggs laid. Adults change into land dwellers in 2-3 years.

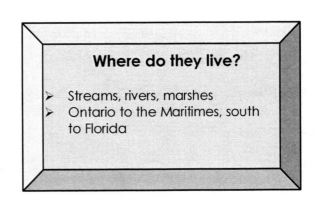

Where do they live?

➤ Streams, rivers, marshes
➤ Ontario to the Maritimes, south to Florida

Did You Know...

◆ During breeding season, males have white lower eyelid glands
◆ If touched by the head or body of a garter snake they remain immobile; if touched by the tongue they jump and flee
◆ Tail is **fragile**
◆ **Hibernate** in streams; **migrate** away from them in the spring and back again at the end of summer
◆ **Nocturnal**, but may be active during rainy summer days
◆ Good swimmers and may be found in fast running streams
◆ Eggs are attached to the underside of rocks in flowing streams and guarded by the female until they hatch
◆ Often collected as fish bait by humans
◆ Eat primarily insects

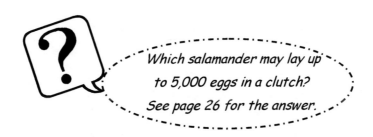

Which salamander may lay up to 5,000 eggs in a clutch? See page 26 for the answer.

Redback Salamander Salamandre rayée
Plethodon cinereus

These are the most widespread and commonly seen salamanders in eastern Canada. They have survived over a wide area because they can tolerate cooler temperatures. Living only on land, they spend the day hiding in woodland debris.

Size 5-10 cm

Colour
Brown with orange or red back stripe, or black with gray back stripe

Reproduction
Up to 25 eggs laid underground. No **aquatic** larval stage.

Where do they live?
- Hardwood forest
- Southern Ontario to the Maritimes, south to Indiana

Did You Know...

◊ Individuals may also be bright red with no stripe, or gray with a black stripe

◊ Can release their tail if threatened; tail that grows back is lighter in colour than the original

◊ Enter backyards and take cover under firewood or boards

◊ **Nocturnal**, searching for food at night and seeking cover during the day

◊ Males will fight for nest sites, marking **territory** with scent marking and fecal pellets

◊ **Hibernate** as deep as one metre in the ground, below the frost level

◊ Diet is mainly insects

◊ Mate in the fall and eggs are laid the following spring

◊ Female lays eggs every other year, and guards them until they hatch

◊ Home range is about 13 square metres for males, and 24 square metres for females

◊ Known lifespan up to four years

Spring Salamander *Salamandre pourpre*
Gryinophilus porphyritcus

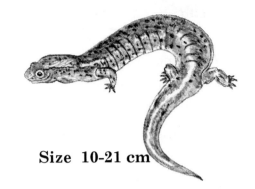

These are among the largest members of this family. Their tail has a knife-like edge on top to aid swimming. They live in mountain springs or other cool, clear waters and use their wedge-shaped head to push between rocks for food.

Size 10-21 cm

Colour
Salmon to red or brown, dark flecks, blotches or bars

Reproduction
Around 100 eggs hatch in 2-3 months. Change into adults in 3-4 years.

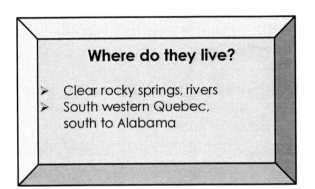

Where do they live?

➤ Clear rocky springs, rivers
➤ South western Quebec, south to Alabama

Did You Know...

◆ Purple colour of the young led to their former name of Purple Salamander.

◆ Bright colour is an indicator of **toxic** skin secretions

◆ Older and larger individuals are darker in colour

◆ Ecology is poorly known

◆ May leave the water at night in heavy rains to look for food on land

◆ **Nocturnal** and semi-**aquatic**, spending most of their time in the water

◆ Prey on other salamanders

◆ Eggs are attached under logs or large rocks in flowing water

◆ Illegal to keep them as pets in Quebec

◆ Known lifespan up to eighteen years

Special Concern

**Loss of habitat
Predation by
introduced fish**

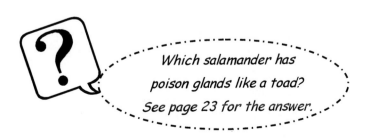

Which salamander has poison glands like a toad? See page 23 for the answer.

Wandering Salamander Salamandre errant
Aneides vagrans

*These long-legged animals are agile climbers, and have been found six metres high in trees. Their **prehensile** tail aids climbing, and they have long, slender digits with well developed pads for gripping. Their eggs have also been found in trees.*

Size 5-10 cm

Colour
Dark brown with no markings, or greenish gray with gold markings

Reproduction
15-20 eggs hatch in 55-60 days. No **aquatic** larval stage.

Where do they live?

➢ Humid coastal forest
➢ Coastal islands of British Columbia, south to California

Did You Know...

◆ Formerly called Clouded Salamander
◆ Juveniles are deep chocolate brown with a bronze back stripe
◆ Tail is round, and tapers to a blunt tip
◆ Skin secretions thought to be **toxic**
◆ Have a defence posture of raising the body and lashing the tail around, followed by flipping around and 'freezing' in place
◆ Feed on insects, spiders and centipedes
◆ Inhabit coastal rainforests up to 1,600 metres
◆ Population density is higher in old growth forests
◆ Active all summer, even during dry periods
◆ Spend the dry season deep within rotten logs in open clearings
◆ Males are sexually mature at two years, females at three years
◆ Males mate every year, females every other year, due to the length of time spent guarding the **clutch**
◆ Eggs are laid individually on the roof or sides of a dark cavity

Western Redback Salamander Salamandre à dos rayé
Plethodon vehiculum

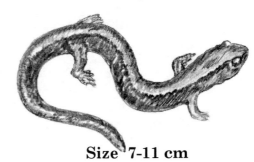

Western Redback Salamanders have stouter bodies and stronger limbs than the similar Eastern species, but are equally common throughout their range. They don't travel long distances, and have home ranges of only a few square metres.

Size 7-11 cm

Colour
Brown or black, yellow, gray or tan back stripe

Reproduction
10-20 eggs hatch in 2-3 months. No **aquatic** larval stage.

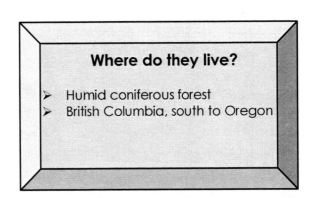

Where do they live?
- Humid coniferous forest
- British Columbia, south to Oregon

Did You Know...

- Individuals with no back stripe may sometimes be found, coloured red, yellow, green or tan
- Belly has salt and pepper flecks
- Most numerous and wide ranging salamander in the west
- Found from sea level to 1,250 metres
- Active at night or during heavy rains; spend the day under logs or stones
- Inhabit damp rockslides and shaded ravines
- Males produce **sperm** every year, but females only lay eggs every other year
- Sexually mature in two to three years
- Breed in the spring and hatchlings emerge in the fall
- Also found on Vancouver Island, BC
- Known lifespan up to eleven years

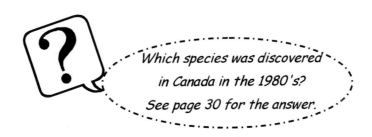

Which species was discovered in Canada in the 1980's? See page 30 for the answer.

Mudpuppy and Waterdog Family
Proteidae

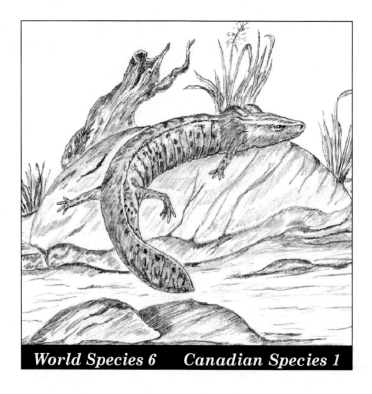

World Species 6   Canadian Species 1

Family Range

This family is represented by five species in North America and one, the cave-dwelling Olm, in Europe.

Characteristics

Mudpuppies and Olms are permanent, water-dwelling **larvae** with both **gills** and lungs. They have long, stout bodies with short tails and large heads. Adults have crimson red feathery **gills** that extend from each side of the head, which is flattened to help them remain on the bottom in fast running water. The tail is flattened from the side to help them swim. They have no eyelids.

Reproduction

Courtship and mating take place in the fall, and the following spring the female prepares a nest cavity in shallow water under logs or rocks. Eggs are laid individually, and attached to solid objects. The female stays with the eggs until they hatch. They cannot breed until they are five years old.

Mudpuppy Necture tacheté
Necturus maculosus

*Mudpuppies are known for their permanent external **gills**, which indicate the temperature and oxygen content in the water. Animals in cold, clear, water have shorter **gills**, while those in warm muddy water with less oxygen have larger ones.*

Size 20-43 cm

Colour
Gray or rusty brown with dark blue spots, bright red external gills

Reproduction
Up to 200 eggs hatch in 5-9 weeks. Adults remain in **neotenic** state their entire lives.

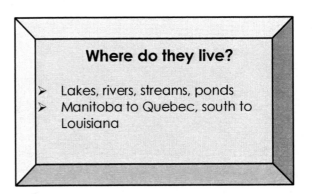

Where do they live?

➤ Lakes, rivers, streams, ponds
➤ Manitoba to Quebec, south to Louisiana

Did You Know...

◈ Largest salamander in Canada, one was recorded at 48 centimetres long
◈ Dull body colours help their **camouflage** on river bottoms
◈ Young are black with yellow stripes running down their body
◈ Spotting pattern varies, with spots sometimes merging to form stripes
◈ Voice is a small squeak barely audible to human ears
◈ Do not **hibernate**, are active all winter and have been found at a record 27 metres
◈ **Nocturnal**, but may be active during the day in murky water
◈ Often caught by ice fishermen, who leave them on the ice to die as they are thought to eat sport fish; there is no evidence to support this
◈ In the mistaken belief that they could bark, they became known as Mudpuppies or Waterdogs
◈ Feed on worms, crayfish, insects and small fish
◈ Are locally abundant but solitary and rarely seen
◈ Have been introduced into large New England rivers
◈ Known lifespan up to twenty-five years

Frogs and Toads

FROGS AND TOADS

Frogs and toads are the largest group of amphibians, and are found all over the world. They are used in scientific study at every stage of their lives. The eggs are used for the study of **embryo** development; **tadpoles** are studied for limb re-growth; and the adults are used in biology courses.

These animals are excellent indicators of the health of their ecosystem, as adults and **larvae** occupy different levels in the food chain. The cause of any deformities can be narrowed down to either the water or the land, making it easier to treat the problem.

FROGS	TOADS
• found in or near water	• live on land
• smooth, moist skin	• dry warty skin
• long hind feet for leaping	• shorter legs for hopping
• fully webbed toes	• little or no webbing

Habitat

Frogs and toads live in a wide variety of habitats, from deserts, mountains and prairies to forests of all kinds. They have developed spectacular adaptations to survival in harsh climates. Some prairie species get most of the water they need through an absorbent patch on their stomach, which they press onto dew-laden plants or into small puddles. Others have adapted to hot, dry areas by burrowing into the soil and forming protective cocoons around their body which keep moisture in. Many species are **freeze tolerant.**

Features

Easily recognized by their body shape, these animals have a squat body, large head, prominent eyes, no tail and back legs which are longer than the front ones. This shape gives them a slanted appearance when sitting. Their sticky tongue is attached at the front, and quickly flipped out to capture insects or other creatures.

When prey is in their mouth, they blink to push their eyeballs down. This increases the pressure in the mouth and helps them swallow. Frogs are more active hunters than toads, who usually sit and wait for their prey to come within reach. Toads also push larger prey species into the mouth with their front legs.

Family Life

In the cooler **temperate regions**, mating occurs in the early spring, with males of many species gathering at ponds and vocalizing. Each species produces its own call, which is timed between the rest spaces of the others so they do not overlap. This produces the familiar chorus effect of continual sound.

Normally only the males have a breeding call, but both sexes may have release and defense calls. Frogs and toads cannot tell males from females by sight, and in the frenzy of mating males will climb on the back of any nearby animal. If they clasp another male or a female who is not ready to mate, a release call is given and the clasping male lets go. Some species give a loud cry when grabbed by a predator.

Egg masses containing many hundreds of eggs are laid on the surface of the water, or attached to submerged vegetation. No parental care is given in the Canadian species, and the **tadpoles** fend for themselves from the moment they hatch.

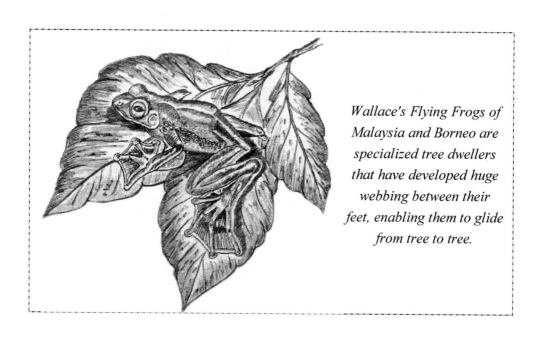

Wallace's Flying Frogs of Malaysia and Borneo are specialized tree dwellers that have developed huge webbing between their feet, enabling them to glide from tree to tree.

Fabulous Frogs !

The Paradoxical Frog of South America goes from a giant, 16 cm **tadpole** to a tiny 5-6 cm frog.

▼

The Golden Poison-arrow Frog is the most **toxic** in the world. An average adult has enough poison in their body to kill nearly 1,000 people.

▼

Glass Frogs of Central and South America have transparent skin on their bellies, and all bones, muscles and organs can be clearly seen.

▼

The longest jump ever recorded was over 5 metres, by the tiny 5 cm Sharp-nosed Frog of South America.

▼

The Common Toad has the record for the highest altitude, being recorded at 8,000 metres in the Himalayan mountains.

▼

The Cane or Marine Toad lays the most eggs of any Anuran—from 30,000 to 35,000 per clutch.

▼

The Australian Water-holding Frog secretes a special outer layer of skin which acts as a cocoon, allowing them to remain buried for years until the rains return.

▼

Skin secretions of the African Clawed Frog contain antibiotics which protect them from bacteria in the ponds and puddles where they live.

▼

The smallest toad in the world is the Oak Toad, measuring just 3 cm. The largest frog in the world is the 30 cm Goliath Frog. Both live in Africa.

▼

Leaf Frogs of Central and South America lay eggs in folded leaves over water, and empty their bladders over them to keep them moist.

▲

Tailed Frog Family

Ascaphidae

World Species 2   Canadian Species 2

Family Range

These highly aquatic frogs are found only in western North America, and rarely stray far from water. Their closest relatives are a small family of tailed frogs found only in New Zealand.

Characteristics

Their skin can be either smooth or warty, and varies from gray, green, reddish or brown to nearly black. Breeding males have hardened black pads on their front feet, arms and chest. They do not possess a true tail, but have a large appendage at the rear end used for fertilizing the eggs. They also have tiny, tail-wagging muscles, a remnant of their ancestors who did possess tails.

Reproduction

Unlike most frog species, the Tailed Frog breeds in fast flowing streams, so internal **fertilization** is necessary to keep the **sperm** from being swept away from the eggs. A few large eggs are laid every other autumn under rocks, and **tadpoles** have sucker-like mouths for clinging to underwater surfaces.

Tailed Frogs Grenouille-a-queue

Tailed frogs require cool mountain streams and are greatly affected by logging, as the disappearance of the trees increases the water temperature. Small, isolated populations have disappeared from logged areas, and re-colonization may take up to 40 years. There are two species in Canada, in two separate areas of British Columbia.

Size
3-5 cm

Colour
Brown, reddish or gray, with dark spots and blotches

Reproduction
Up to 75 eggs laid. Adults appear in 5 years.

Where do they live?

➤ Clear, swift flowing streams
➤ See details below.

Coast Tailed Frog
Ascaphus truei

Range:
Coastal mountains of British Columbia, south to California

Special Concern

Rocky Mountain Tailed Frog
Ascaphus montanus

Range: Interior mountains of British Columbia, south to Idaho

Endangered

Did You Know...

◈ Active day or night, when temperature, humidity are right
◈ Only Canadian frog that does not have a mating call; they cannot hear airborne sounds so males visually search for females in breeding season
◈ One of the least tolerant frogs to dry conditions
◈ Only lay eggs every other year; have the largest eggs and longest **embryo** development time of any frog in North America
◈ **Larvae** feed on algae and conifer pollen, which they scrape off submerged rocks
◈ Do not breed until seven or eight years of age
◈ Are not found on Vancouver Island, or other western coastal islands

Treefrog Family

Hylidae

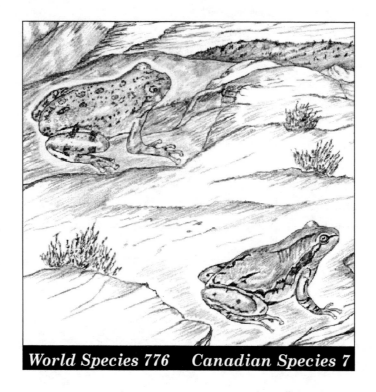

World Species 776   Canadian Species 7

Family Range

Treefrogs are widespread throughout North, Central and South America, with the largest number in the tropics. They are also found in northwestern Africa, Eurasia, Australia and New Guinea.

Characteristics

Most, but not all, members of this family live in trees. Their toe pads are larger than those of other species, with circular, sticky pads used in climbing. Their long, slender toes can swivel backwards and sideways to grip branches. Many species have bright **flash colours** on the underside.

Reproduction

Breeding habits vary greatly in this large family. While most lay their eggs in ponds or streams, some of the tropical species go to marvellous lengths to reproduce. Females may carry their eggs on their back in a mass of jelly, or in a temporary pouch formed by a fold of skin. The smallest species lay eggs inside plants growing high up on trees.

Chorus Frogs

These frogs may be heard calling in early spring, even before the ice has completely disappeared. Silent males will often sit close to calling ones during mating season, to intercept females attracted by the calls. Their voice has been compared to a fingernail running over the teeth of a comb.

*The Boreal species differs from the Western in that they have very short hind legs, so they hop but cannot jump. They can best be told apart by their location, as their Canadian ranges do not overlap. Both species are **freeze tolerant**.*

Size
2-4 cm

Colour
Brown, green or reddish, with three dark back stripes

Reproduction
100-800 eggs laid. Adults appear in 3-4 months.

Where do they live?
- Bogs, marshes, ponds, lakes
- See details below

Boreal Chorus Frog Rainette faux-grillon boréale
Pseudacris maculata

Range: Northwest Territories, north western British Columbia, Alberta to Ontario, south to Illinois

- Smallest frog in Canada
- Rarely climb above the tops of tall grasses
- Disappear beneath the water surface at the slightest disturbance
- Males have rasping call that is often assumed to come from larger frog
- Will breed in any pond with at least ten centimetres of water
- Population is largest on the southern prairies
- Known lifespan up to three years

→

Western Chorus Frog Rainette faux-grillon de l'ouest
Pseudacris triseriata

Range: Southern Ontario and Quebec, south to Georgia

◈ Skin is moist and bumpy
◈ Males have yellow **vocal sac** that looks like a loose flap of skin
   when they are not calling
◈ Females are larger than males
◈ Frequently inhabit the shoreline instead of staying in
   the water
◈ Rate of development of eggs and **larvae** is dependent on
   water temperature
◈ Survive near large cities where their loud chorus can be heard on spring nights
◈ Found throughout central to eastern portions of the continent
◈ Were introduced into Newfoundland in the 1960's, but population there has since
   died out

What's In A Name?

Some other definitions for frog in the English language:

piece of foam used to keep flower arrangements in place;
piece on the end of a violinist's bow;
tender horn in the middle of a horse's foot;
loop fastening on a coat, used instead of a button;
clasp on a belt for carrying a sword or bayonet;
grooved section of metal to keep trains on the rails at intersections.

Gray Treefrogs

*In appearance, these two frog species are identical, but their calls and Canadian ranges are different. The two species are found together only along the Red River in Manitoba. Both species are **freeze tolerant**, and can tolerate temperatures as low as −29°C.*

*Gray treefrogs can change their colouration from gray to brown to green in minutes. Low temperatures cause their **pigment** to expand and the skin becomes darker; higher temperatures produce the opposite effect. Bright light will cause the skin to turn pale, while less light causes it to darken. Newly changed adults are bright leaf green.*

Size
3-5 cm

Colour
Greenish or brownish gray, belly bright yellow or orange

Reproduction
Up to 2,000 eggs hatch within a week. Adults appear in 2-3 months.

Where do they live?

➢ Vegetated ponds, marshes
➢ See details below

Cope's Gray Treefrog Rainette criarde
Hyla chrysoscelis

Range: South eastern Manitoba, south western Ontario, south to Florida

◈ Skin is rougher than other frogs; sometimes called Tree Toads
◈ **Tadpoles** have bright orange or red tails
◈ Call is a hearty, resonating trill heard spring and summer
◈ Attracted to walls or windows at night because of the insects gathered there
◈ Males each have a **territory** 75 cm or more from each other and engage in wrestling matches to defend them
◈ Known lifespan up to six years

→

Eastern Gray Treefrog Rainette versicolore
Hyla versicolore

Range: Southern Manitoba to Quebec, New Brunswick, south to Florida

◈ Can be found at the top of the tallest trees
◈ Rarely seen outside of the breeding season
◈ Prefer mature, old growth forest
◈ Males call from trees and shrubs, but enter water to mate
◈ Female selection of a mate is influenced by the duration of their calls, and how many nights they participate in the chorus
◈ Eggs are laid on the water surface, among vegetation
◈ Known lifespan up to four years

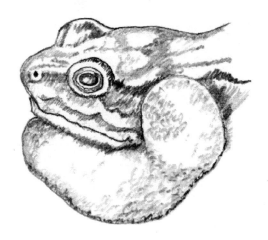

*Three different types of **vocal sacs**, inflated for calling.*

Northern Cricket Frog Rainette grillon
Acris creptians

A fairly common species until the early 1970's, the population of these frogs then began to decline rapidly. Once found throughout southern Ontario, it is not known if any still remain in that province. They are numerous in the USA.

Size 1-4 cm

Colour
Greenish, gray or brown, dark triangle between the eyes

Reproduction
200-400 eggs laid.
Adults appear within one season.

Where do they live?

➤ Vegetated ponds, slow streams
➤ South western Ontario, south to Texas

Did You Know...

◆ Have a warty appearance, an elongated snout and lots of webbing on the hind feet; head has a distinctive triangle mark

◆ Voice sounds like a metallic 'gick gick', resembling steel marbles, or the winding of a watch

◆ Difficult to catch as they hop among grasses right at water's edge

◆ A non-climbing member of the treefrog family

◆ Can jump more than a metre; escape predators by jumping in zigzag motions

◆ **Hibernate** away from water under rocks, logs or in holes

◆ Hatch and change into adults within one season

◆ Very short lifespan, living as adults for only one breeding season

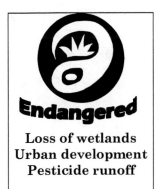

Endangered

**Loss of wetlands
Urban development
Pesticide runoff**

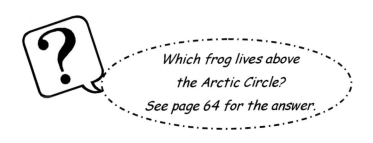

Which frog lives above the Arctic Circle?
See page 64 for the answer.

Pacific Treefrog Rainette du Pacifique
Hyla regilla

The distinctive 'rivet' or 'ribbet' call of this little frog has been heard around the world. When moviemakers want an authentic outdoor sound, this is the call they use for tropical noises in films and cartoons, to typify a frog sound.

Size 2-5 cm

Colour
Green, tan, red, blackish with darker markings

Reproduction
Up to 70 eggs hatch in 3-5 weeks. Adults appear in their first summer.

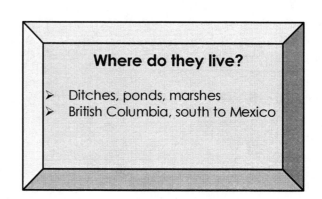

Where do they live?

➢ Ditches, ponds, marshes
➢ British Columbia, south to Mexico

Did You Know...

◆ Most abundant amphibian in the northwest USA
◆ Change colour rapidly from light to dark shades, depending on the moisture and temperature of their surroundings
◆ Females are larger than males
◆ Sticky feature of their toes is being studied by researchers with the aim of providing new technology for car tires
◆ Live on the ground among vegetation, always near water
◆ Active day and night
◆ Silent males locate themselves near calling males to intercept females during breeding season
◆ Native American tribes believed that an individual treefrog co-exists for every person, thus these frogs were shown great respect
◆ Also found on Vancouver Island, BC and have been introduced to Graham and Queen Charlotte Islands
◆ Population is declining throughout their range due to poor water quality

Spring Peeper Rainette crucifère
Pseudacris crucifer

One of the more familiar species in the east, the chorus of these frogs is often one of the first signs of spring. Beginning on the first warm nights, the volume increases with every warm spell. By May, it can become so loud it hurts the human ear.

Size 2-3.2 cm

Colour
Brown, greenish or gray, dark cross on back

Reproduction
1000-5000 eggs hatch in 2 weeks. Adults appear in 2-3 months.

Where do they live?

➤ Ponds, swamps, marshes
➤ Manitoba to the Maritimes, south to Florida

Did You Know...

◆ Able to change colour from light to dark shades and back again
◆ Throat of the males is dark with light yellow flecks during breeding season
◆ Can jump 17 times their body length
◆ Males sing in trios; the one who starts usually has the deepest voice
◆ Named for their piping whistle of one repeated note
◆ Home range 1.2-2.5 metres; daily travel ranges from 6-39 metres
◆ **Freeze tolerant** species
◆ Chorus is said to sound like the jingling of sleigh bells from a distance
◆ Can be found **foraging** in the forest outside of breeding season
◆ **Hibernate** on land
◆ Feed only on soft-bodied prey: spiders, moth larvae etc.
◆ One of the earliest breeders in the spring
◆ Known lifespan up to two years

True Frog Family

Ranidae

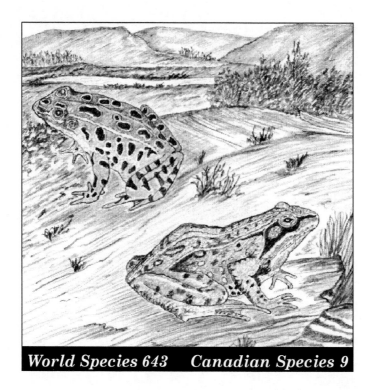

World Species 643   Canadian Species 9

Family Range

This family is found around the world, except for Greenland, Antarctica, New Zealand and Madagascar. They are advanced frogs with many different lifestyles.

Characteristics

Generally large frogs, adults divide their time between the land and water. Their head is usually somewhat pointed, the eyes and external eardrum are large. Their long, muscular legs are well suited for both jumping and swimming. The Canadian species can be divided by colour and pattern: brown frogs, green frogs and boldly spotted frogs.

Reproduction

Early breeders lay masses of eggs in cool, highly oxygenated water. Later breeders lay a film of eggs on the surface, as there is less oxygen in warmer water. The egg masses are laid close together by several females, forming a large mass. This is likely an adaptation to the climate, as the small black **embryos** absorb heat from the sun and the thick jelly acts as an insulator. The temperature in the egg mass may be 6°C warmer than that of the surrounding water.

Bullfrog Ouaouaron
Rana catesbeiana

The largest frogs in North America, these animals weigh up to 0.5 kg, and are a favorite species for **culinary** *frog's legs. Attempts to harvest them have led to many introductions outside their range, where they are rapidly depleting the smaller frogs.*

Size 9-13 cm

Colour
Green to yellowish brown

Reproduction
Up to 25,000 eggs laid
on water surface. Adults
appear in 2-3 years.

Where do they live?

- Ponds, lakes, slow streams
- Ontario to the Maritimes, south to the Gulf Coast

Did You Know...

- ◇ Named for their call which sounds like the bellowing of a bull; the deep 'jug-o-rum' can be heard up to one kilometre at night
- ◇ **Hibernate** by burying themselves in mud at the bottom of water bodies and building a protective cave-like cavity
- ◇ Adult males aggressively defend a **territory** of 3-25 metres
- ◇ **Cannibalistic** and will eat smaller frogs; large specimens eat small birds and young snakes
- ◇ **Tadpoles** may be three centimetres long with four legs before their tail has been absorbed; look like a cross between a frog and a salamander
- ◇ In 1949, a 3.25 kilogram individual was caught in Washington State
- ◇ Legal to hunt them in Ontario outside breeding season; only 15 can be taken daily, and a license is required to sell them in some parts of the province
- ◇ Have been introduced to British Columbia, Vancouver Island, western USA, Hawaii, Jamaica, Italy and Japan.
- ◇ Known lifespan up to 14 years

Green Frog Grenouille verte
Rana clamitans

Like a few others of the family, female green frogs choose which male they mate with based on the desirability of his **territory** *for egg laying. Males establish a breeding area 1-6 metres in diameter and defend it throughout the breeding season.*

Size 5-9 cm

Colour
Green, yellow or brown

Reproduction
Up to 7000 eggs laid.
Adults appear the
following summer.

Where do they live?

➢ Brooks, swamps, ponds, lakes
➢ South eastern Manitoba to the
  Maritimes, south to the Gulf Coast

Did You Know...

◆ Males have a bright yellow throat, and swollen thumbs for clasping the female
◆ Many limb deformities reported for this species
◆ Produce as many as six different calls, one of which sounds like a note struck on a loose banjo string
◆ **Hibernate** in water at the bottom of the pond
◆ Males defend a **territory** of four to six metres at their breeding site
◆ May disperse up to five kilometres from where they changed into adults
◆ **Tadpoles** overwinter in mud at pond bottom
◆ Hunted for **culinary** frog's legs and dissection in school classes
◆ Widespread throughout eastern North America; have been introduced to British Columbia, Newfoundland, Washington, Utah and Hawaii
◆ Known lifespan up to eight years

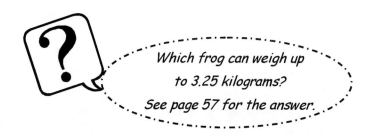

Which frog can weigh up to 3.25 kilograms?
See page 57 for the answer.

Mink Frog Grenouille du nord
Rana septentrionalis

These are the only known frogs that emit a distinct
odour. They produce a pungent, musky scent that
has been compared to that of the mammal mink, or
rotten onions, when handled. It is thought to be a
chemical defense to deter predators.

Size 4-9 cm

Colour
Olive to brown, dark
spots and blotches

Reproduction
500-1500 eggs laid.
Adults appear the
following summer.

Where do they live?

➤ Cold vegetated lakes and ponds
➤ Manitoba to the Maritimes, south
  to Minnesota

Did You Know...

◆ One of the few amphibians with the largest part of their range in Canada
◆ Highly **aquatic**, and seldom found on land
◆ Call sounds like two sticks being struck together; a large chorus sounds like popcorn
  popping or distant hammering
◆ Usually found where water lilies are abundant, as they can hunt from the leaves and
  remain out of reach of fish
◆ Males call while floating on the water
◆ **Nocturnal** and extremely wary
◆ Males spend the night squatting on lily pads far from shore
◆ Require habitat where vegetation is abundant
◆ **Tadpoles** overwinter in bottom pond mud

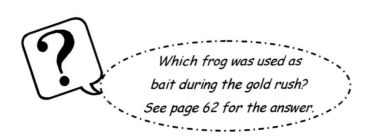

*Which frog was used as
bait during the gold rush?
See page 62 for the answer.*

Northern Leopard Frog Grenouille leopard
Rana pipiens

An absorbent pelvic patch allows these frogs to live away from water. By keeping this patch in contact with the ground they absorb any moisture from dew or raindrops. They are usually found in short grass meadows where there are lots of insects.

Size 5-9 cm

Colour
Brown, bronze, or green,
with round black spots

Reproduction
2000-4000 eggs laid. Adults
appear late summer.

Where do they live?
➤ Marshes, sloughs, ponds
➤ NWT, south western BC, Alberta to
the Maritimes, south to Nebraska

Did You Know...

◆ Also called Meadow or Grass Frog, Shad Frog or Herring Hopper
◆ Found as far north as Ft. Smith, NWT, and have been introduced to
Vancouver Island, BC
◆ When pursued on land, they flee in zigzag leaps to water; can
jump fifteen times their body length
◆ Call is usually given as they float spread-eagled on the surface,
but they may call from underwater
◆ Often squawk if startled, or even scream when caught
◆ **Migrate** over a wide area between feeding, breeding and
hibernation sites
◆ The most often used species in biology courses
◆ Larger specimens are collected for the frog leg market; collected
commercially for fishing bait; froglets also used as bait for fishing
◆ Population has declined rapidly in British Columbia and the prairies; eastern
population is not at risk
◆ Known lifespan six years

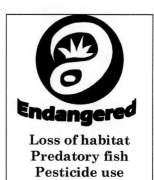

Endangered
Loss of habitat
Predatory fish
Pesticide use

Pickerel Frog Grenouille des marais
Rana palustris

One of the few poisonous frogs in North America, these animals produce **toxic** *skin secretions that make them unappetizing to predators. They are avoided by frog eating snakes, and can be fatal to other amphibians kept in the same terrarium.*

Size 4-8 cm

Colour
Yellow, tan or bronze with square dark markings

Reproduction
Up to 2000 eggs laid.
Adults appear the
following summer.

Where do they live?

➢ Slow moving water, ponds
➢ Southern Ontario to Maritimes, south to Texas

Did You Know...

◆ Have parallel rows of dark, squarish spots on back
◆ Inner side of legs is bright yellow or orange
◆ Voice is a steady low croak like the lowing of a cow; may call in a rolling snore underwater
◆ **Hibernate** in bottom mud sediment
◆ Interbreed with Northern Leopard frogs, and the two species are often confused
◆ Hunt for food in meadows and fields
◆ Have been introduced to Newfoundland
◆ Used as bait for fishing; name may have originated from the custom of using them to fish for pickerel
◆ Have been found living in caves in the USA
◆ Known lifespan up to four years

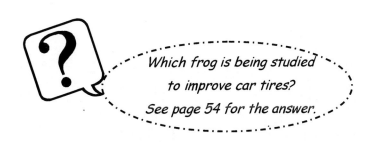

Which frog is being studied to improve car tires?
See page 54 for the answer.

Red-legged Frog Grenouille à pattes rouges
Rana aurora

Males of this species have been known to clasp almost anything in breeding season: other frog species, salamanders and even apples. Females get rid of unwanted males by extending their legs and rolling on their sides.

Size 7-10 cm

Colour
Reddish brown, olive or gray with pinkish colour inside the legs

Reproduction
500-1000 eggs laid.
Adults appear in 2-3 months.

Where do they live?

➢ Temporary ponds, lakes, marshes
➢ British Columbia, south to California

Did You Know...

◆ Toes are not fully webbed
◆ May stray 200-300 metres from standing water into fields
◆ Often call underwater, which is barely audible at the surface; call given above water carries only 10 metres
◆ Collected for **culinary** frog leg market
◆ Used as bait by fishermen since the gold rush of 1849
◆ Have been introduced to one county in Nevada, and they are common throughout their USA range
◆ **Tadpoles** develop faster in warmer water
◆ Population is declining on Vancouver Island, due in part to the introduced Bullfrogs
◆ Known lifespan up to fifteen years

Loss of habitat
Predation by
introduced frogs

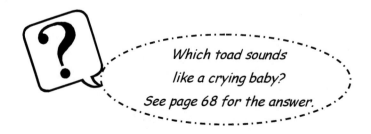

Which toad sounds like a crying baby?
See page 68 for the answer.

Spotted Frogs

These two frogs have many similarities but live in separate ranges. They inhabit cool, mountainous waters with little vegetation, and are not found in warmer waters that allow extensive plant growth.

Size
7-10 cm

Colour
Brown, greenish, reddish
or gray, dark spots with
light centres

Reproduction
Up to 1500 eggs laid.
Adults appear the
first summer.

Where do they live?

➢ Cool streams, ponds, lakes
➢ See details below

Columbia Spotted Frog
Grenouille maculée de Columbia
Rana luteiventris

Range: Southern Yukon, British
Columbia, south western
Alberta, south to Montana

Oregon Spotted Frog
Grenouille maculée de l'Oregon
Rana pretiosa

Range: South western British
Columbia, south to Idaho

Endangered

Did You Know...

◆ Have bright **flash colours** of red and white
◆ Mating call is low and carries only 20-30 metres
◆ Call is a series of short, rapid grunts
◆ When frightened, they swim to the bottom and remain still
◆ Eggs of many females may be deposited on top of each other, until the mass rises above the water surface
◆ Oregon Spotted only known at three sites in Canada
◆ Have difficulty surviving where Bullfrogs have been introduced
◆ Threatened by loss of habitat and draining of the wetlands
◆ Known lifespan (Oregon Spotted) six years

Wood Frog Grenouille des bois
Rana sylvatica

*Wood frogs live further north than any other amphibian in North America. A **freeze tolerant** species, they can remain frozen at –3°C for several weeks. Up to 65% of their body fluids freeze, and they are able to thaw and freeze repeatedly.*

Size 3.5-7 cm

Colour
Brown, olive, gray or near black, with black facial mask

Reproduction
500-1100 eggs hatch in 1-2 weeks. Adults appear in 2-3 months.

Where do they live?

➢ Ponds, streams, lakes
➢ Alaska, Yukon, NWT, Alberta to Maritimes, south to Alabama

Did You Know...

◆ Can change colour shade from light to dark in fifteen minutes
◆ Only North American frog north of the Arctic Circle; range extends to the treeline
◆ Can be identified by their black facial patch; called the frog with the 'robber's mask'
◆ Scatter into woodlands after breeding, which explains their name
◆ Those in eastern Canada have longer legs than those in the west
◆ Call is a low, rapid, duck-like quacking
◆ Only member of this family to **hibernate** on land
◆ Are explosive breeders; swarms of pairs lay eggs within 1-2 days then return to the forest
◆ Earliest amphibian to breed, often calling while snow and ice remain
◆ Jelly around the egg mass turns green with the presence of algae, which provides temperature protection and **camouflage**
◆ Have been introduced into western Newfoundland

True Toad Family
Bufonidae

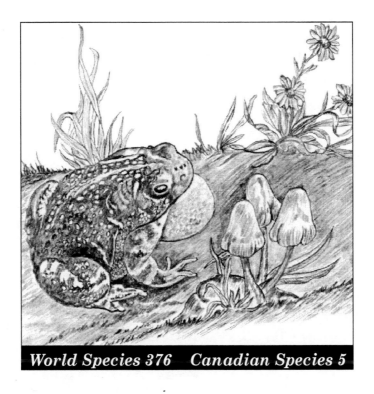

World Species 376   Canadian Species 5

Family Range

True toads are native to all continents except Australia, New Zealand, Madagascar, Antarctica and Greenland. One species, the Cane Toad *(Bufo marinus),* was introduced to Australia in 1935 and continues to wreak havoc on native species.

Characteristics

Although toads have a similar body shape to frogs, their skin is dry, rough and warty. This helps reduce water loss, so toads have been able to colonize more arid areas. Their large bladder is used for water storage. All members of this family have large **parotoid glands** on their shoulders. If picked up in a predator's mouth, a white milky secretion oozes from these glands, poisoning the animal. Some animals seem immune to this secretion - garter snakes, water snakes and hognose snakes all prey on toads with no ill effects. Birds and mammals have learned to leave the skin, and eat the meat to avoid the poison. Humans can also be affected if the eyes are rubbed after touching a toad.

Reproduction

Eggs are laid in the water in one or two long strings. Their development is rapid, and young toadlets that leave the water in summer may triple in size by the autumn.

American Toad Crapaud d'Amérique
Bufo americanus

*These are the only toads in most of eastern Canada. Busy eaters of insects and other small **invertebrates**, they are welcome backyard visitors. It has been estimated that one toad will eat more than **9,000** insects over the summer.*

Size 5-9 cm

Colour
Brown, gray, green, reddish, black with darker blotches

Reproduction
Up to 12,000 eggs hatch in 1-2 days. Adults appear in 2-3 months.

Where do they live?
- Ponds, lakes, streams
- Manitoba to the Maritimes, south to Georgia

Did You Know...

◆ **Tubercles** on the hind feet are used to dig themselves backwards into soil; spend the day in burrows

◆ Poison from **parotoid glands** can temporarily paralyze a dog's respiratory system

◆ Voice is pleasant musical trill, sometimes lasting up to half a minute

◆ Chorus day and night in breeding season; males each select a different note for their call

◆ Temperature affects the mating call; the cooler the temperature, the longer the call

◆ Have a defensive posture of sprawling on their back and playing dead

◆ In breeding frenzy, males have been known to clasp a rock, a boot or even a dead fish

◆ **Tadpoles** also have poison glands in their skin

◆ Found as far north as James Bay, ON

◆ Known lifespan up to thirty-six years

Canadian Toad Crapaud de Canada
Bufo hemiophrys

Similar in appearance, habitat, and calls to the American Toad, these toads have one or two large bony humps between the eyes. It is these crests that distinguish them. The two species are known to interbreed.

Size 5-8 cm

Colour
Brown, gray, greenish or rust with brownish red spots

Reproduction
Up to 7000 eggs hatch in 3-12 days. Adults appear in 6-7 weeks.

Where do they live?

➤ Shallow lakes, ponds
➤ NWT, Alberta, Saskatchewan, Manitoba, south to Minnesota

Did You Know...

◈ One of the few amphibians with most of its distribution in Canada
◈ Large spots have many small warts inside them
◈ **Tubercles** on the hind feet are used for digging
◈ Call is a weak, low pitched trill repeated every 15-20 seconds
◈ Have heavily spotted bellies
◈ Found as far north as Ft. Smith, NWT
◈ Burrow underground to avoid extreme summer heat
◈ **Hibernate** below the frost line
◈ Active day or night, depending on the temperature
◈ Readily take to water to avoid capture
◈ Males may call at temperatures as low as 5°C

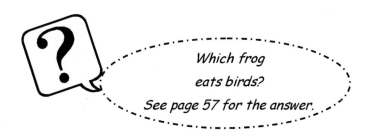

Which frog eats birds?
See page 57 for the answer.

Fowler's Toad Crapaud de Fowler
Bufo fowleri

These little toads inhabit open sandy areas near marshes, lakes and ditches. Loose sand is essential to their survival, as they burrow into it during hot, dry periods, and in winter. They are threatened by the recreational use of beaches.

Size 5-8 cm

Colour
Gray, tan, or olive, dark blotches and one dark spot on belly

Reproduction
3000-10,000 eggs laid.
Adults appear their
first summer.

Where do they live?

➤ Backwater marshes
➤ Shoreline of Lake Erie, ON, south to the Gulf Coast

Did You Know...

◆ Previously considered a subspecies of Woodhouse's Toad
◆ Throat of the male turns black in breeding season
◆ Call sounds like the crying of a baby
◆ Species relies on shorelines, which are altered by severe storms
◆ If roughly handled, they may lie on their back and pretend to be dead
◆ Sometimes **hibernate** in groups in underground chambers
◆ Eat almost exclusively insects
◆ Cool weather may disrupt the breeding season, with young being born and changing into adults at different times
◆ **Tadpoles** use tooth-like structure to scrape algae off rocks
◆ Known lifespan up to four years

Threatened
Loss of habitat
Pesticide use

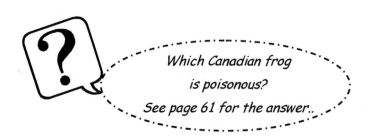

Which Canadian frog is poisonous?
See page 61 for the answer..

Great Plains Toad Crapaud des steppes
Bufo cognatus

Dry-land toads require habitat with loose soil where they can easily burrow to escape hot, dry conditions. These toads construct shallow burrows that are level with the surface by backing into the ground with shuffling motions of their hind feet.

Size 5-11 cm

Colour
Gray, olive or brown,
large dark blotches

Reproduction
Up to 20,000 eggs hatch
in about 2 days. Adults
appear in 6-7 weeks.

Where do they live?

➤ Sloughs, ditches, flooded fields
➤ Southern Alberta, Saskatchewan, south western Manitoba, south to Mexico

Did You Know...

◈ Belly is pure white
◈ **Vocal sac** of males looks like a loose flap of black skin when they are not calling; inflates to a large, tubular shape which bends up and over the top of their nose
◈ Call sounds like a pneumatic drill and may carry two kilometres across the prairies; longest call of any frog or toad, lasting several minutes
◈ Have a defensive posture of inflating the body to appear larger, closing the eyes and lowering the head to the ground
◈ Usually **nocturnal**, but may be active on cloudy or rainy days
◈ Breeding occurs in response to heavy rains
◈ Active predator of cutworms, which cause extensive crop damage; their value to agriculture has been estimated at $25 for each animal
◈ Threatened by the use of agricultural chemicals
◈ Live on the disappearing short grass prairie
◈ Illegal to keep them as pets in Alberta
◈ Known lifespan up to ten years

Endangered

**Loss of habitat
Pesticide use
Extended drought**

Western (Boreal) Toad Crapaud de l'ouest
Bufo boreas

*Mainly **nocturnal** at lower elevations, Western Toads hunt throughout the day at higher, cooler altitudes. They can be found in forests up to 3,000 metres. Dry periods are spent in burrows which are either self-dug, or have been abandoned by others.*

Size 6-12 cm

Colour
Green to brown, white or yellow back stripe

Reproduction
Up to 17,000 eggs hatch in 3-12 days. Adults appear in 6-8 weeks.

Where do they live?

➢ Ponds, streams, rivers, lakes
➢ Alaska, NWT, Yukon, British Columbia, Alberta, south to Baja

Did You Know...

◈ Do not have the cranial crests found on other toads
◈ Reddish-brown warts are surrounded by black marks
◈ Call sounds like the weak peeping of baby chicks, and is rarely heard
◈ Only true toad found in British Columbia
◈ Tend to walk rather than hop
◈ Defensive posture of rising up on their legs and puffing the body up to make themselves look larger
◈ **Tadpoles** school together, swarming from place to place to stir up food from the bottom
◈ Increased UV radiation decreases hatching success of eggs
◈ Found in the boreal forest
◈ Known lifespan up to six years

Special Concern

Urban development
Draining wetlands
Introduced fish

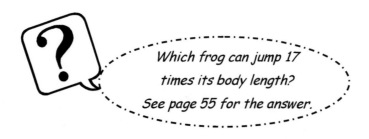

Which frog can jump 17 times its body length? See page 55 for the answer.

Spadefoot Toad Family
Pelobatidae

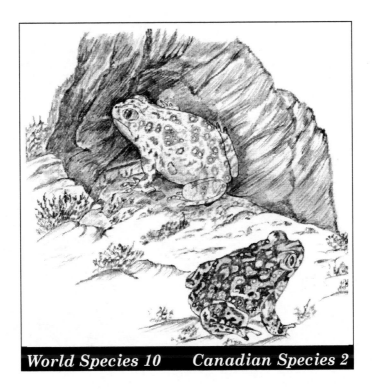

World Species 10   Canadian Species 2

Family Range

This family of plump, specialized toads is found in the prairies, deserts and steppes of North America, Europe, northwest Africa and Asia.

Characteristics

Their name comes from a sharp-edged 'spade', or **tubercle**, on the hind feet, which is used to burrow into loose soil. Living in hot, dry areas, they spend the day underground, and can survive losing nearly half their body weight through moisture loss. They rarely come out during daylight hours, except in heavy rains. They are different from true toads because they have teeth on their upper jaw, smoother skin and no poisonous **parotoid glands** on the shoulders.

Reproduction

These toads breed when heavy spring rains arrive. Eggs are laid in clusters, and attached to underwater vegetation or pebbles. As they breed in temporary water that may quickly dry, these toads have very rapid development. The time from the laying of the eggs to development into adults can be as little as two weeks.

Great Basin Spadefoot Toad Crapaud du Grand Bassin
Spea intermontanus

Lacking the warty skin of true toads, these animals are relatively smooth skinned. Their short snout is slightly up-turned, giving them a pug-nosed appearance. Unlike the Plains Spadefoot, these toads have a soft, not bony, hump on the head.

Size 3-6 cm

Colour
Brown, gray or olive, with dark markings on back that may form an hourglass.

Reproduction
300-800 eggs hatch in 2-7 days. Adults appear in 6-8 weeks.

Where do they live?

➢ Temporary pools, slow streams
➢ Southern British Columbia, south to New Mexico

Did You Know...

◆ Voice is a series of short, hoarse, rapid calls
◆ **Migrate** several hundred metres between breeding and feeding areas
◆ Usually **nocturnal**, but may hunt during cloudy or rainy days
◆ Mating call is a loud *gwaah* repeated over and over
◆ Spend long periods underground during dry spells
◆ Inhabit sagebrush flats, semi-desert scrub and woodlands
◆ May be brought to the surface by driving or stamping near their burrow; it is thought they mistake the vibrations for heavy rain
◆ Look like pebbles when sitting still
◆ Known lifespan up to ten years

Threatened

**Loss of habitat
Urban development
Herbicide use**

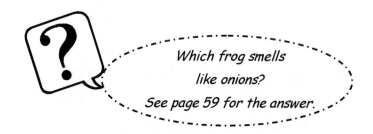

Which frog smells like onions?

See page 59 for the answer.

Plains Spadefoot Toad Crapaud des plaines
Spea bombifrons

The self-dug burrows of these toads range from a few centimetres to several metres, and the entrance remains open. Adhesive material is occasionally found at the entrance, which is thought to cement the loose soil in place and prevent collapse.

Size 4-5 cm

Colour
Gray, brown or greenish,
may have light coloured stripes

Reproduction
Up to 200 eggs hatch in
48 hours. Adults appear
within 2 months.

Where do they live?
➤ Temporary pools, slow streams
➤ Southern Alberta, Saskatchewan,
   Manitoba, south to Texas

Did You Know...

◈ Have a bony, elevated hump between the eyes called a 'boss'
◈ Small warts are tipped with orange or yellow
◈ Skin secretions smell somewhat like garlic
◈ Mating call sounds similar to the quack of a duck
◈ Found on the disappearing short grass prairie
◈ Vertical pupils like a cat indicate a **nocturnal** lifestyle
◈ Newly changed adults may disperse a kilometre or more from where they hatched
◈ Lay their eggs in any available water, even cattle tanks
◈ **Tadpoles** will eat anything, even each other; an adaptation to quick
   development in arid areas

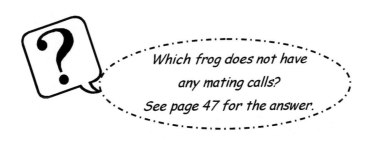

*Which frog does not have
any mating calls?*
See page 47 for the answer.

Reptiles

Laying hundreds of eggs in water works well for the amphibians, but to live on land a different method had to be developed. Eggs had to be resistant to drying out, so a solid shell had to be provided. With their evolutionary advantages of hard skin and shelled eggs, reptiles have colonized land, trees, underground and water habitats the world over. They are found on every continent except Antarctica. Living reptiles are divided into four **Orders**, two of which, turtles/tortoises and lizards/snakes are found in Canada. The remaining two – crocodilians and the tuatara – live in more tropical areas.

The Outside Story

One big difference between reptiles and amphibians is their skin. Reptiles do not breathe through their skin, so it has thick layers that protect the body and keep moisture in. Their outer skin is made of keratin, the same substance that makes up horns, antlers and hooves, as well as human nails and hair. The scales covering their body are connected by hinges and often overlap. Unlike fish scales, those of reptiles are not separate, but form one continuous sheet. They can be smooth, granular or keeled, which means they have ridges running lengthwise.

Like the amphibians, reptiles are always growing, and must shed their skin every so often. Some shed in pieces, but snakes usually shed their entire skin in one piece. They rub the scales free from the mouth area, then crawl forward so the skin comes off in one single inside-out piece. People used to think they shed once a year, but it really depends on how much they eat and how fast they grow.

The Wet Look

Reptiles are not slippery and wet like amphibians. They have dry skin which is fairly warm to the touch. Their colour and pattern is determined by the type and arrangement of **pigment** cells. All colours except blue and green are formed on the inner layer of the skin and not on the scales. The scales themselves are clear, and it is light hitting these scales that gives them a 'wet look'. Some species are **iridescent**, and have shimmering, changing colours like a rainbow.

Ovi or Ovo

With hard shelled eggs, reptiles had to develop a method of fertilizing the eggs before the shell formed. They use internal **fertilization**, with the **sperm** being introduced directly into the female by specialized organs.

Reptile eggs can be soft and leather-like, or hard like those of birds. They are laid in warm, moist areas such as mammal burrows, thick vegetation, sawdust, decaying logs or even the foundations of old buildings. Development varies with the temperature; the warmer they are, the faster they develop. There is no larval stage, and the newborns are miniature versions of their parents. The eggs contain a large yolk sac to nourish the growing **embryo**, and the young have a temporary egg tooth to cut the shell open. The babies develop into a tight spiral, so hatchlings may be up to seven times longer than the egg that held them.

Many species of lizards and snakes do not lay eggs, but carry the eggs inside their body and give birth to live young. These animals are called *ovoviviparous*. This is common in the cool, **temperate regions** of the world. Females are better able to regulate the **incubation** temperature if growth occurs inside the body. Live bearers only reproduce every second or third year. Females give birth late in the summer and may not be able to obtain enough food before **hibernation** to reproduce the following year. Reptiles that lay eggs are called *oviparous*.

> *The United Nations has estimated that the damage done by rodents worldwide amounts to 42.5 million tonnes of food, roughly the same as the world's total annual production of cereals and potatoes. Reptiles help control their populations.*

The Special Tongue

Snakes and lizards often wiggle their forked tongue in the air. They do this to 'read' or sense their surroundings. Each side of the fork senses the direction of, and distance to, the odour. Scents and other chemical molecules gathered on the tongue are brought back into the mouth through a small notch in the upper lip. A pair of sensitive cells called the *Jacobson's Organ* examines these scents, and sends signals to the brain. Different from smell or taste, this organ gives them a more complete picture of their surroundings. It is only found in amphibians, lizards and snakes. People used to think these flicking tongues were poisonous, but they are harmless in all species.

Defence Masters

Reptiles have developed a wide variety of defense methods, with **camouflage** being the most important. Turtles can withdraw their soft body parts inside their shells. Many lizard species have **fracture points** in their tails, which can be broken off if grabbed by a predator. Snakes and lizards also use fleeing, playing dead or aggressive displays. Many snakes will discharge a foul smelling scent from their **anal gland** if roughly handled. Vipers have **toxic** venom, which is used as a last resort. All reptiles like to avoid contact with humans, and prefer to escape as fast as they can.

Friend or Foe

Lizards and snakes live on the species man calls pests. Insects, mice, rats, ground squirrels and voles make up most of their diet. Some fish, birds, amphibians and other reptiles are also taken. Hunting is done by sight and smell, with prey being actively chased. Food is swallowed whole.

Turtles and tortoises are well liked by man, snakes are universally feared or hated, and lizards are generally tolerated. It is a great pity that people do not realize these animals are a very important part of any healthy ecosystem.

Mohawk Indians respected the Snapping Turtle above all other creatures, and their leading clan was that of the turtle.

*

Nootka Indians of the west coast related snakes to lightening, perhaps because of their quickness.

*

In ancient Japan, turtles were considered symbols of happiness and good fortune because of their long lives.

*

Hawksbill Turtle shells were valued by ancient Egyptians for jewellery and knife handles.

*

In Asia, it is considered good luck if a geckco barks while a child is being born.

*

In India, people once believed a lizard's wisdom was in its tongue. Children ate the tongues so they would grow up clever and well spoken.

*

Iroquois believed the serpent was the god of fire and on ceremonial occasions they danced with a snake in their hands.

*

Snakes represented healing to the ancient Greeks and knowledge to the Incas.

*

Turtles are still revered in parts of India, and kept in temples and shrines.

Turtles and Tortoises

TURTLES AND TORTOISES

Turtles have changed little in the last 200 million years, and have been on earth since before the dinosaurs. As anyone who has watched a turtle knows, they have a very low **metabolic rate**, and move very slowly. Their activity level and growth rate is slow, and they have very long life spans. Records include 120 years for the European Pond Turtle, and 138 years for the North American Box Turtle.

Habitat

Turtles live in almost every habitat, on every continent except Antarctica, and in all oceans of the world. Land dwellers are generally called tortoises, while the **aquatic** species are called turtles or terrapins.

Their feet and limbs indicate the type of habitat where they live, and how they move. Land-dwelling tortoises have elephant-like feet with no webbing, while species in freshwater have long, webbed toes. The feet of the ocean dwellers have adapted to flipper-like limbs.

Features

Among the most recognizable creatures in the world, these animals all have bodies enclosed in a shell, and four short limbs. The shell is covered with horny plates known as **scutes,** or leathery skin, which gives them their colour and design. Land turtles usually have high domed shells as a defense against the jaws of predators. Marine species have lower, flatter shells to reduce water resistance.

The upper part of the shell is called a **carapace**, the lower is called the **plastron**. A bridge on each side of the body joins the two. The spinal column and rib cage are attached to the **carapace**. Only their neck, legs and tail are able to move freely. Because their ribs are joined to the upper shell, they cannot expand their rib cage to breathe. Muscles in the abdomen expand and compress the lungs by pushing internal organs against them.

> **Aquatic** turtles can also breathe through their skin and the lining of the throat. Some larger species can survive for weeks underwater.

Turtles do not have teeth, but use a sharp, horny bill to tear their food. Their diet varies, with most species eating both plants and animal matter. The largest species in the world, the Leatherback Sea Turtle, lives mainly on jellyfish.

Their vision is excellent, and they are able to tell colours apart. With external ears protected by membranes, they are able to hear airborne sounds. They have upper and lower eyelids. Unlike other reptiles, their tongue is not forked, and cannot be extended beyond the mouth.

Family Life

Basking in the sun is very important to turtles that live in water, and they usually begin their day this way. The temperature of the water does not rise as quickly as that of the air. To rapidly raise their body temperature, they must **bask** on a rock or log above the surface. The sun not only raises their body temperature, but provides Vitamin D, which contributes to the health of their shell.

Turtles must come on land to lay eggs. Females dig a nest in soft soil, lay the eggs, cover them up and leave. No parental care is given, and the young fend for themselves from the moment they hatch. The temperature around the eggs dictates the sex ratio of the young in many species. Higher temperatures usually produce more female offspring. In Canada and other **temperate regions**, eggs may not hatch at all if the weather is too cool.

The Big-headed Turtle of Asia is unable to retract its head inside the shell, so both the head and tail are covered with armoured scales.

Terrific Turtles !

The Black Soft-shelled Turtle of Bangladesh has the
most limited range of any, and is found only at one
shrine, in a 50 metre wide pond.

▼

The Pancake Tortoise and Big-headed Turtle are
among the few species that lay only one egg.

▼

Leopard Tortoises of Africa, moved up to 13 kilometres,
returned to their original area within 14 days.

▼

The fastest documented swimming speed for a
sea turtle was a Pacific Ridley at
35 kilometres per hour.

▼

Desert tortoises have been known to drink over 40%
of their own body weight in just over an hour.

▼

In ancient China, the markings on the shell were
believed to foretell the future to those who could
read them.

▼

Horsfield's Tortoise of Kazakhstan is active only
three months of the year. The remaining nine
months are spent buried underground.

▼

The oldest documented lifespan for a tortoise is
152+ years for an Aldabra Giant Tortoise.

▲

Snapping Turtle Family
Cheldridae

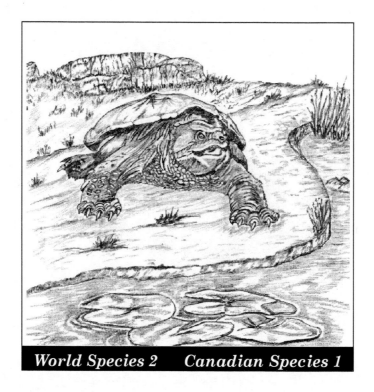

World Species 2   Canadian Species 1

Family Range
This family of aggressive fresh water turtles is found only in North, Central and South America.

Characteristics
Among the largest freshwater turtle species, they can grow up to 46 centimetres long, and weigh up to 22 kilograms. Snapping Turtles are known for their quick tempers, and can strike with amazing speed. Their large heads cannot be fully retracted into their shell. They have powerful hooked jaws that can cut through flesh, and easily remove a human finger or toe. Their long tail has a series of bony plates, giving it a toothed appearance. These turtles like to rest in warm shallow water, often buried in the mud with only their eyes and nostrils exposed. Older individuals often have shells covered with algae, which makes them harder to see in the water.

Reproduction
Eggs are laid in a deep cavity, with each one being directed into place by alternate movements of the hind feet. In cooler regions, hatchlings may spend the winter in the nest, and climb out in spring.

Common Snapping Turtle Chélydre serpentine
Chelydra serpentina

Due to their large size, Snapping Turtles are often hunted for food, and trapped and sold to the restaurant trade. Some people consider them a delicacy, and soups and stews are made from their flesh. Their eggs are also collected for food.

Size 20-50 cm

Colour
Tan, dark brown
or black

Reproduction
20-50 eggs hatch
after 9-18 weeks

Where do they live?

➢ Ponds, marshes, shallow lakes
➢ South western Saskatchewan to Maritimes, south to the Gulf Coast

Did You Know...

◈ Canada's largest freshwater turtle; record weight is 22 kilograms
◈ Name comes from the sound of their jaws snapping shut
◈ Excellent swimmers; have found their way back several hours after being moved over three kilometres
◈ Sometimes eat ducklings and goslings, grabbed from below
◈ Small prey is swallowed whole; larger items are held in the mouth and torn to bits with their long front claws
◈ Females may retain **sperm** in their bodies for many years before laying eggs
◈ **Incubation** temperatures of over 30°C or below 20°C mean offspring will be female; temperatures in between produce males
◈ Shells were once used as ceremonial rattles by Native Americans
◈ Known lifespan up to 57 years

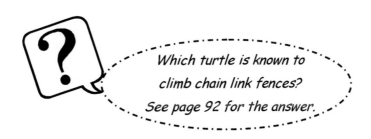

Which turtle is known to climb chain link fences?
See page 92 for the answer.

Mud and Musk Turtle Family
Kinosternidae

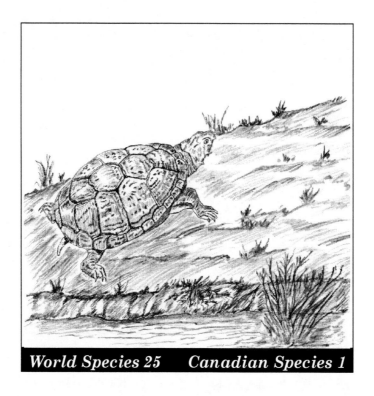

World Species 25   Canadian Species 1

Family Range
These highly **aquatic** turtles are found in North, Central and South America.

Characteristics
These feisty little turtles have elongated heads, and fleshy bulges hanging on their chin. Older individuals may have shells covered with algae, which helps **camouflage** them on the bottom of ponds. They have two pairs of **musk glands** that produce a foul smelling liquid if they are threatened. The **plastron** has either one or two hinges, which means they can partially close their shell. The tail of the males is much longer than that of the females, and ends in a spine-like nail.

Reproduction
Females in warmer areas usually lay more than one **clutch** per year of eggs with delicate, porcelain-like shells. Canadian species generally lay only once per year. The eggs may be light pink, bluish, white or have bands of a darker cream.

Common Musk Turtle Tortue musquée
Sternotherus odoratus

*Musk turtles prefer shallow water with little or no current. Although highly **aquatic**, they are poor swimmers, and prefer to walk on the bottom, probing the mud with their heads to look for food. They eat, mate and **hibernate** in the water.*

Size 7-13 cm

Colour
Olive brown to dark gray, with black markings

Reproduction
Less than 10 eggs hatch after 9-12 weeks

Where do they live?

➢ Slow water, shallow ponds
➢ Southern Ontario, south to the Gulf Coast

Did You Know...

◈ Also called Stinkpot, or Stinking Jim
◈ Newly hatched young are about the size of a nickel
◈ Juveniles have spots or streaks on their **carapace**
◈ Powerful jaws can inflict a painful bite
◈ Produce a musky scent when threatened
◈ Active morning and evening, spend the day buried in mud
◈ Rarely come to shore to **bask**; float on the water surface or sit in shallow water
◈ Good climbers, and can climb slanted trees to two metres above the water surface
◈ Do not dig a nest to lay their eggs; use a shallow depression or muskrat lodge
◈ Sometimes take bait off fishermen's lines
◈ **Hibernate** in groups
◈ Known lifespan up to 53 years

Threatened
Shoreline development Boat traffic

Pond, Marsh and Box Turtle Family
Emydidae

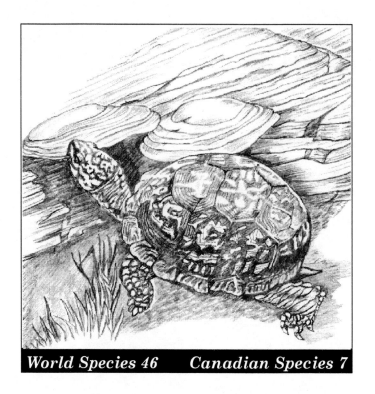

World Species 46   Canadian Species 7

Family Range
This is the largest turtle family, and the most familiar to people. They live in The Americas, Europe, Asia and northwest Africa.

Characteristics
These are small to medium size turtles with bony, **scute** covered shells that are slightly flattened. Their colour varies throughout the family, and there are usually stripes and patterns on the legs and head. These animals spend only part of their time in the water, and their hind feet are flattened and partially webbed. Box turtles have two hinges on their **plastron**. This means they can completely close their protective shell with their soft body parts tucked safely inside.

Reproduction
They have an elaborate **courtship** behaviour, with the male facing the female and stroking her head and neck with his long front claws. Northern species nest only once per season, while those in more southerly areas may nest two or three times a year. Hatchlings of many species in the **temperate regions** overwinter in the nest, and emerge the following spring.

Blanding's Turtle Tortue mouchetée
Emydoidea blandingi

*These turtles could be called semi-box turtles.
Their hinged **plastron** allows the front half to
close tightly, but the back shuts only part way. The
pattern on the upper shell resembles duckweed,
which aids their **camouflage**.*

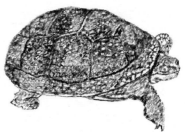

Size 12-26 cm

Colour
Blue black **carapace**,
bright yellow chin and throat

Reproduction
20-22 eggs hatch
after 3-4 months

Where do they live?

➢ Ponds, marshes, shallow lakes
➢ Southern Ontario and Quebec,
Nova Scotia, south to Nebraska

Did You Know...

◆ Only turtle in Canada with a bright yellow chin and throat
◆ Have a long neck, flat head and bulging eyes
◆ Range limited to Great Lakes region of North America, with a
  small population in Nova Scotia
◆ Feed in the water, but come ashore to **bask**
◆ Very tolerant of cold temperatures
◆ Require shallow waters with lots of vegetation
◆ Timid and not aggressive
◆ **Hibernate** in the mud on pond bottoms or in muskrat lodges
◆ Females do not mature until 14 years of age
◆ Gender of offspring determined by **incubation** temperature
◆ Named for a herpetologist in the USA in the early 1800's
◆ Often killed on roads while searching for food
◆ Known lifespan up to 30 years

Threatened
Loss of habitat
Urban development

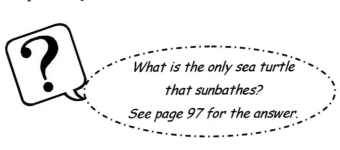

*What is the only sea turtle
that sunbathes?*
See page 97 for the answer.

Box Turtle Tortue tabatière
Terrapene carolina

Box turtles are the longest-lived species of North American wildlife. It was once popular to carve the date in their shell, and dates found on one turtle indicated an apparent lifespan of 138 years. They are found only in North America.

Size 10-21 cm

Colour
Black or brown, with
yellow or greenish markings

Reproduction
5-7 eggs hatch
after 2-3 months

Where do they live?

➤ Open woodlands, meadows
➤ South western Ontario, south to Alabama

Did You Know...

◈ Males have red eyes, while females' are dark brown

◈ May spend their entire lives in an area about the size of a football field

◈ Mainly **terrestrial**, but seek out water bodies during dry spells

◈ Have been observed feeding on a dead cow

◈ Able to eat mushrooms that are poisonous to man

◈ **Hibernate** on land, digging into dirt or debris and going deeper as the temperature drops

◈ Sexually mature in five to seven years

◈ Females can store **sperm** and reproduce several years after mating

◈ Gender of offspring determined by **incubation** temperature in the nest

◈ Native Americans ate their meat, used the shell for ceremonial rattles and buried them with their dead

◈ Unknown if any still live in Canada, but are abundant in the USA, and often kept as pets there

◈ Known (documented) lifespan 100 years

Common Map Turtle Tortue géographique
Craptemys geographica

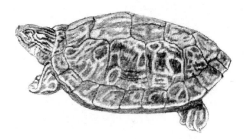

*A series of thin yellow lines on the **carapace** of these turtles resemble the lines on a map. This pattern is more noticeable on younger animals, and may disappear entirely in adult females. The head and legs also have bright yellow lines.*

Size 10-27 cm

Colour
Greenish to olive brown, with thin yellow lines

Reproduction
12-14 eggs hatch after 3-4 months

Where do they live?
➤ Slow moving rivers, lakes
➤ Southern Ontario and Quebec, south to Alabama

Did You Know...

◆ Female's large crushing jaws can break open clams and snails; smaller males eat insects and small **invertebrates**

◆ **Gregarious**, may be seen stacked atop one another while basking on logs or rocks

◆ Food is always swallowed underwater

◆ Shy and elusive, retreating into water at the slightest noise

◆ Eggs are deposited in double layers with some earth in between

◆ Gender of offspring is determined by **incubation** temperature in the nest

◆ Female covers the nest with soil, then rubs it with her **plastron** to smooth it

◆ Sexual maturity not reached until ten years of age

◆ Known lifespan up to 20 years

Special Concern
Loss of habitat
Urban development

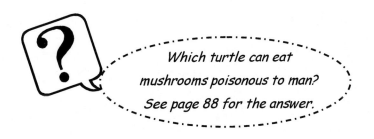

Which turtle can eat mushrooms poisonous to man? See page 88 for the answer.

Painted Turtle Tortue peinte
Chrysemys picta

The most common and widespread turtle in Canada, these animals are found across the southern portion, with the exception of the hot, arid prairie region. They are also found throughout much of the eastern and midwestern USA.

Size 10-25 cm

Colour
Olive to black, with yellow and/or red markings on body

Reproduction
Up to 20 eggs hatch after 10-11 weeks

Where do they live?

➢ Slow streams, rivers, ponds
➢ British Columbia to the Maritimes, south to Georgia

Did You Know...

◈ Also called a Mud Turtle

◈ Cold tolerant species; can survive temperatures as low as -9°C and may be seen swimming under the ice

◈ Dozens may be observed basking together on a single log

◈ Active during the day and sleep at night among vegetation or on pond bottom

◈ **Hibernate** by burying themselves up to 45 centimeters deep in soft mud at the pond bottom

◈ Nesting females often killed by automobiles as they search roadsides for nesting areas

◈ Gender of offspring is determined by **incubation** temperature in the nest

◈ Sexual maturity reached at five years for males, eight years for females

◈ Young are **carnivorous**, but change their diet to plants as they mature

◈ Known lifespan up to 40 years

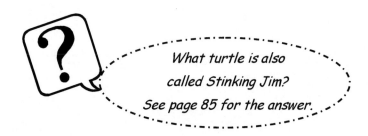

What turtle is also called Stinking Jim?
See page 85 for the answer.

Spotted Turtle Tortue ponctuée
Clemys guttata

*The dark **carapace** of these turtles is covered with bright yellow spots. The number and size of these spots varies considerably, and may be red, orange or yellow. Females have yellow chins and orange eyes, while males have a tan chin and brown eyes.*

Size 8-14 cm

Colour
Black or bluish black
with round yellow spots

Reproduction
3-5 eggs hatch
after 3-4 months

Where do they live?

➢ Bogs, shallow lakes, marshes
➢ Southern Ontario and Quebec, south to Florida

Did You Know...

◆ Sometimes called Cranberry Turtle, for their fondness for living in these bogs
◆ Can be found sunning themselves in large groups during the cooler months
◆ Have favourite basking sites, which they return to repeatedly
◆ **Hibernate** in groups in bottom mud, or muskrat burrows
◆ Avoid extreme sun and long dry periods by burrowing into dense underwater vegetation
◆ May be found **foraging** in wet grasses
◆ Require undisturbed quiet water with some vegetation
◆ Favourite food is insects
◆ Deaths due to road kills and raccoon predation are on the increase
◆ Known life span up to 42 years

**Loss of habitat
Poaching for
pet trade**

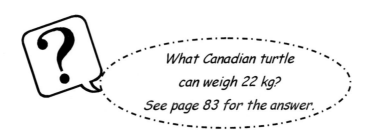

What Canadian turtle can weigh 22 kg?
See page 83 for the answer.

91

Wood Turtle *Tortue des bois*
Clemmys insculpta

Wood turtles are thought to be one of the most intelligent turtles. In laboratory tests, they scored as high as white rats. They can be seen searching for worms in freshly plowed fields, and have been known to scale a 1.8 metre chain link fence.

Size 12-23 cm

Colour
Brown or gray, with reddish neck and forelegs

Reproduction
6-18 eggs hatch after 4-5 months

Where do they live?

➤ Deciduous forest, wet meadows
➤ Southern Ontario to the Maritimes, south to Virginia

Did You Know...

◆ Hearing is said to be similar to that of a cat
◆ Shell has a rough appearance, with each **scute** showing prominent growth rings
◆ Semi-**terrestrial**, and only completely submerge during **hibernation**
◆ Have been seen stomping on the ground to imitate rain and bring worms to the surface
◆ **Courtship** ritual includes male and female facing each other and swinging their heads from side to side
◆ Wander a considerable distance from water in the summer and often soak in mud puddles
◆ Once popular as food, they are now suffering from over-collection for the pet trade
◆ Known lifespan up to 60 years

Special Concern
Poaching for pet trade
Habitat loss

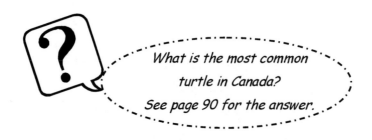

What is the most common turtle in Canada? See page 90 for the answer.

Softshell Turtle Family
Trionychidae

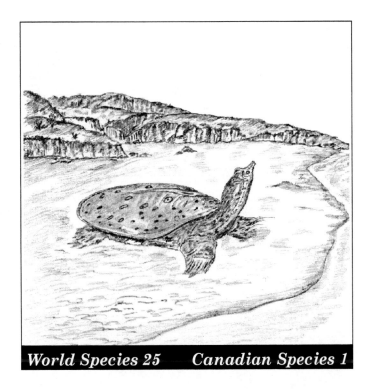

World Species 25   Canadian Species 1

Family Range
These unusual turtles have a wide distribution, and can be found in North America, Africa and tropical Asia.

Characteristics
Easily identified by their shell, it is nearly circular in shape and covered with a soft, leathery skin instead of bony **scutes**. They have a narrow head with a tube-like snout, and a long neck. Their jaws are razor sharp. Their feet are paddle-like, fully webbed, and the front limbs have three long, sharp claws. Strong swimmers, they often swim beneath the water surface, with just their snouts sticking out of the water. They can survive long periods underwater, and breathe through their skin as well as their mouth.

Reproduction
Mating takes place in deep water, and one **clutch** is laid per year in the northern parts of their range. Unlike most turtle species, the gender of hatchlings is not determined by the temperature in the nest.

Spiny Softshell Turtle Tortue-molle à épines
Apalone spinifera

These turtles have a rough textured **carapace** *that is flat, round and leathery. The bones of the shell do not go all the way to the edges, so it is flexible on the sides. There are small spines on the front edge.*

Size 12-45 cm

Colour
Greenish to dark tan
with dark blotches

Reproduction
Up to 30 eggs hatch
after 4-5 months

Where do they live?

➢ Rivers, lakes with soft bottoms
➢ Southern Ontario and Quebec,
  south to the Gulf Coast

Did You Know...

◈ Also called Pancake or Flapjack Turtle
◈ Canada's only freshwater turtle with a leathery **carapace**
◈ Nostrils can close, allowing them to stay underwater for hours
◈ Females are nearly twice as large as the males
◈ Fast moving on land and in water
◈ Bury themselves by flipping silt on their back with their feet
◈ Get almost half their oxygen by breathing through their skin
◈ Spend most of their time **foraging** or floating in the water, or
  buried in mud with just the head and neck showing
◈ Can be aggressive and hard to handle if threatened; large adults
  can bite off a human finger
◈ Hatchlings may overwinter in the nest
◈ Quebec population resides in Lake Champlain; breeds on the Canadian
  side but winters in New York State
◈ Known lifespan up to 25 years

Threatened
Loss of habitat
Urban development
Water pollution

Sea Turtle Family

Cheloniidae

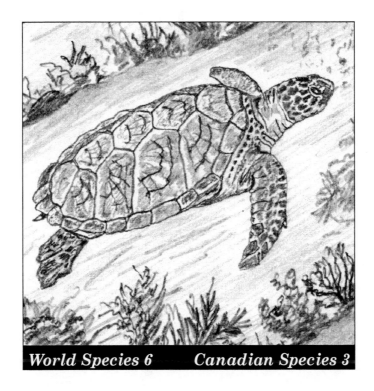

World Species 6   Canadian Species 3

Family Range

These huge turtles are found in all warm oceans of the world. Although they are not officially found in Canada, they sometimes stray into Canadian waters, so have been included here. All are endangered on a world wide basis.

Characteristics

Members of this family all have heart shaped **carapaces**, covered by bony **scutes**. They have paddle-like flippers with one or two claws. The shell is low and streamlined to reduce water resistance, and the head cannot be retracted into the shell. Special glands allow them to drink salt water, and discharge the excess salt.

Reproduction

Their habit of always using the same tropical nesting beaches has made these animals easy prey for man. Once a beach has been identified as a nesting site, people know the animals will return, and the hunt for eggs and meat continues. Females emerge from the ocean in a large group to nest at the same time. Two or three **clutches** of a hundred or more eggs are laid in one to three year cycles. It is thought that only one in 10,000 hatchlings live to reach adulthood.

Atlantic Ridley Sea Turtle   Tortue bâtarde
Lepidochelys kempi

Like all marine turtles, this species is very endangered. They have been nearly wiped out due to egg robbing, slaughter of nesting females, and drowning in shrimp boat nets. They nest only along a short stretch of beach in the Gulf of Mexico.

Size 60-75 cm

Colour
Gray **carapace** and body, pure white underneath

Reproduction
100-150 eggs hatch after 50-70 days

Where do they live?

➢   Atlantic Ocean

Did You Know...

◆ Also called Kemp's Ridley Sea Turtle
◆ Weigh up to 67 kg
◆ Capable of closing their nostrils underwater
◆ Tapping on the shell sounds like tapping on dead wood
◆ Inhabit shallow coastal waters, and are bottom feeders
◆ Courting, mating and egg laying take place in daylight hours
◆ Hatchlings leave the nest in daylight, but not all at the same time
◆ In the past, 40,000 would gather off their nesting beach before coming ashore to lay eggs
◆ Sometimes seen off the coast of Europe and the United Kingdom
◆ May range as far north as Nova Scotia in the summer
◆ Known lifespan up to 16 years

Endangered

Poaching for eggs and meat Loss of nest sites

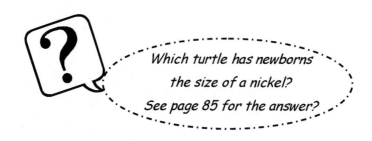

Which turtle has newborns the size of a nickel? See page 85 for the answer?

Green Sea Turtle Tortue verte
Chelonia mydas

Hatchlings of this species spend their first year adrift at sea on floating mats of vegetation. A year later they re-appear in shallow waters, and remain there 20-30 years. Then they return to exactly where they hatched to reproduce.

Size 71-153 cm

Colour
Olive to dark brown,
may have dark patterns

Reproduction
100-180 eggs hatch
after 45-60 days

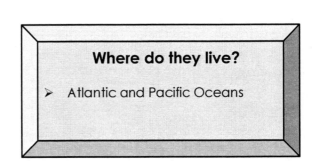

Where do they live?

➤ Atlantic and Pacific Oceans

Did You Know...

◈ Common name comes from the colour of their flesh

◈ Have a heart shaped **carapace**

◈ Tail of the males is tipped with a flattened nail, and extends well beyond the shell

◈ Record weight is 385 kilograms

◈ Swim at 2.4 kilometres per hour

◈ Only sea turtle that sunbathes; sometimes **bask** on the ocean surface, providing a landing spot for seabirds

◈ Feed in shallow seas, may range as far north as the Maritimes

◈ Spend over 90% of their time in water, and can remain submerged up to five hours

◈ Are the only sea turtle that eats mainly plants

◈ Eggs are laid at night; hatchlings emerge at night, all at the same time

◈ Have long been hunted for turtle soup

◈ Reproduce only every two or three years

Endangered
**Poaching for
eggs and meat
Loss of nest sites**

Loggerhead Sea Turtle Caouane
Caretta caretta

Loggerheads migrate 10,000 kilometres from their hatching sites to feed off the coast of Baja, Mexico. They take two years to make the trip, feed and grow for five years, and then make the journey back to reproduce where they hatched.

Size 79-122 cm

Colour
Reddish brown

Reproduction
100-130 eggs hatch
after 7-9 weeks

Where do they live?

➤ Atlantic and Pacific Oceans

Did You Know...

◆ Named for their large chunky head, which has powerful jaws for crushing hard prey

◆ Largest hard-shelled turtle in the world; known to reach 2.7 metres but their usual size is closer to 90 centimetres

◆ Historical records show 455 kilogram specimens, but are usually around 136 kg

◆ Have been seen as far as 300 km from shore; enjoy floating on the ocean surface

◆ An estimated 14,000 nest in the southeastern USA annually

◆ Eggs are about the size of ping-pong balls; newly hatched young are about five centimetres long

◆ Hatchlings attracted to the light reflected off the ocean are sometimes confused by highway lights, and crawl onto roads

◆ Eat both marine vegetation and animal matter; are immune to the poisonous stings of jellyfish

◆ May range north to coastal Newfoundland in the summer

◆ Known lifespan up to 33 years

Endangered
Poaching for eggs and meat
Loss of nest sites

Leatherback Sea Turtle Family

Dermochelyidae

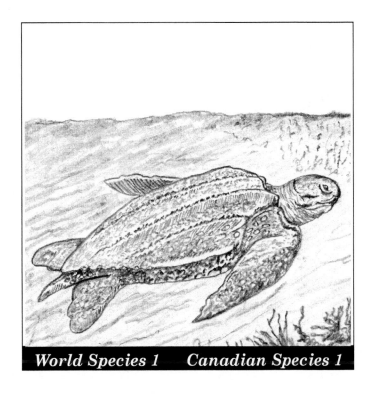

World Species 1   Canadian Species 1

Family Range

Leatherbacks are found in all oceans except the polar areas. They are the largest turtles in the world. Weights of 700 kilograms and lengths of two metres have been recorded. Their front flippers span nearly three metres.

Characteristics

Their shell is covered with smooth, oily, leathery skin. The **carapace** is made up of many small bony platelets embedded in the skin. Because they do not have the rigid shell of other turtles, their ribs and vertebrate are not attached to it. The forelimbs have become large flippers. These animals can regulate their body temperature to a certain degree, and keep their internal temperature warmer than the surrounding sea. This allows them to range further north than other marine turtles.

Reproduction

Up to nine **clutches** may be laid each season, about ten days apart. The nest cavity may be waist high on a man. Before leaving land, the females circle the nest site. When the hatchlings emerge, they too circle the nest site once before heading for the ocean. Egg laying and hatching take place at night.

Leatherback Sea Turtle Tortue luth
Dermochelys coriacea

Little is known of the ecology of these turtles, due to the difficulty of keeping them in captivity. When captured, they flail at their captor with their flippers. If enclosed in a tank, they batter against the sides and thrash around continually.

Size 1.2-2 m

Colour
Slate to blue black or grayish, with white or yellow markings

Reproduction
50-170 eggs hatch
after 8-10 weeks

Where do they live?

➢ All oceans except polar areas

Did You Know...

◈ Have long, backward facing spines in the mouth and throat which help them swallow slippery jellyfish
◈ Often swim in groups in the open ocean
◈ Weak jaws are adapted to soft-bodied prey
◈ **Migrate** north, following jellyfish which are their main prey
◈ Powerful swimmers, and can easily pull a six metre sailboat for several kilometres
◈ Hunted for their oils for cosmetics, and eggs for protein
◈ Documented cases of letting shipwreck survivors hang onto their shell, sometimes for hours
◈ Hatchlings are born with scales on the skin and shell, which disappear in the first two months
◈ Visit coastal British Columbia and the Maritimes summer and fall
◈ Very endangered, due to tourist resort development on their nesting beaches

Endangered
Poaching for
eggs and meat
Loss of nest sites

Lizards

LIZARDS

With over 4,000 species, lizards are the largest living group of reptiles. They may look like salamanders, as most have four limbs and a long tail. However, lizards have dry, scaly skin, clawed feet and external ear openings that the amphibians do not. Like other animals, lizards have been killed by man for centuries for their flesh and eggs.

Lizards are perhaps the most familiar reptiles to people around the world. Active during the day, they range from the Arctic Circle to New Zealand.

Habitat

Lizards live in a wide variety of environments: arid deserts and grasslands, warm oceans and forests of all kinds. They are found on the surface, beneath the ground and in trees. There are more species in the tropical areas, and two **venomous** species in the southern USA and Mexico.

Their body shape is associated with their lifestyle. Those living in dense vegetation or under the sand are long and slender. The slow-moving plant eaters are more heavily built. Some tree-dwelling lizards can glide through the air by extending a flap of skin along each side of their body. Lizards may have four legs, two legs, or no legs at all. The so-called legless lizards look like snakes, but have small remnants of limbs, external ear openings and movable eyelids.

Features

These reptiles cannot open their mouths to eat prey larger than their body. The two halves of their lower jaw are firmly attached, which restricts the size of the items they can eat. Their tongue is attached at the back of the mouth, and can be extended beyond the jaw to capture prey. Most species eat insects, small mammals, birds and other meat. Only 2% of lizard species are plant eaters.

Lizards have a third eyelid, or *nictitating membrane,* which protects their eyes. It covers the eye but is transparent so they can still see. With their eyes placed on the side of their head, they can see above, ahead and to the side. Sight is the most important sense for those that live on land. Their sense of smell is also essential for many species. They are able to pick up ground vibrations, but with external ears they can also hear airborne sounds.

Most lizards walk by moving one front leg and the opposite hind leg forward at the same time, then do the same with the other side. Some have very muscular hind legs and may walk or run with the front feet raised off the ground. Their legs and feet are adapted to their habitat - desert species have scales on their toes to help them walk on hot sand; climbing lizards have sharp claws or gripping pads on their toes.

Tails are used to store body fat, and for swimming, visual displays and balance. Some species have **prehensile** tails. Lizards possess **fragile tails**, which means they are able to drop a portion of the tail if caught by a predator. Their tails have **fracture points** where they break off, and the muscles will contract and neatly separate. They are able to do this more than once, but each re-growth is smaller and lighter than the original tail.

Colour is very important for these animals. Some species blend almost perfectly into their environment, and some have bright **flash colours** on their undersides. In most species the males are more colourful, while the females are better **camouflaged** and more drab. Blending into their environment is the most important method of defense. They may also use sitting still, running, inflating their body and pushing up and down with their legs, jaw gaping, or weaving their tail and head around.

Family Life

Most species have a **courtship** display of ritual fighting among males. They threaten each other with head bobbing, loud noises, changing colour or displaying crests and throat fans. They may lunge forward and act as if they are going to bite. At the start of breeding season, males increase the number of displays to scare other males off their **territory**. The **courtship** only progresses to mating if the female is receptive.

There is little or no parental care of the young, but some species guard the eggs until they hatch. Very few species help the hatchlings emerge from the egg, or defend the newborns from predators.

More than 60 cm long, the Solomon Island Skink is the only member of the Skink family that eats plants, and they rarely come down from the trees.

Legendary Lizards !

The Australian Thorny Devil has channels
between their scales that funnel dew from
their body to their mouth.

▼

The only known **venomous** lizards are the Gila
Monster of the south-western USA and the
Mexican Beaded Lizard, who have
well developed venom glands in the lower jaw.

▼

The Green-blooded Skink of New Guinea has
green pigment in their blood, a green tongue,
and lays green eggs in trees.

▼

The Giant Solomon Island skink bears one live young
that is one third the size of the female.

▼

Central American Indians have always eaten iguanas,
and you can buy iguana burgers in Panama.

▼

Some chameleons are so deaf that shouting next to
them when they're sleeping will not wake them up.

▼

Some skinks have been known to return to the spot
where they lost their tail tips and eat them, a unique
example of self-**cannibalism**.

▼

Male Barking Geckos of Africa chorus
together at night like frogs.

▼

The Common Lizard lives above the
Arctic Circle in Norway.

▲

Iguana Family
Iguanidae

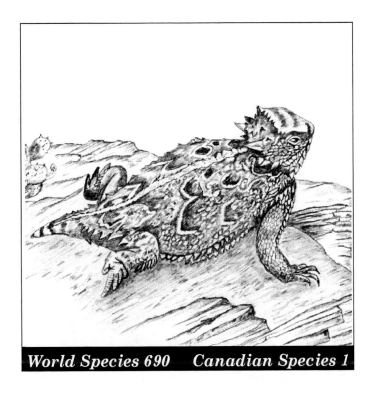

World Species 690   Canadian Species 1

Family Range

Iguanas are a large family, with most living in North, Central and South America. A few species live on the islands of Madagascar, Fiji and Tonga. As a family, they have a huge variety of lifestyles. Some are tree-dwellers with **prehensile** tails; some burrow, and some swim and dive.

Characteristics

These lizards are usually brown, gray, black, bright green or blue. They have throat fans, crests on their back and fringes of scales on their toes. Their tongue is thick, fleshy and grooved at the tip. Limbs are strong and well developed, and they have large, round eyes with noticeable lids.

Reproduction

Males in this family defend a breeding **territory**. They rise up on their front legs, bob their head, extend throat fans and crests, snap their jaws and hiss at intruders. This behaviour is just for display, and actual fights are uncommon. Most members of this family are egg-layers, and the number of eggs varies among species. The Short-horned Lizard is an exception, as they retain their eggs and give birth to live young.

Short-horned Lizard Iguane à petites cornes
Phrynosoma hernandezi

These amazing lizards have a unique defense of squirting blood from their eyes. Thought to result from a rise in blood pressure when threatened, they can rupture a blood vessel in the corner of their eyes, and squirt it as far as two metres.

Size 6-14 cm

Colour
Gray, yellowish or reddish brown, with two rows of dark spots on back

Reproduction
6-30 live young born
July or August

Where do they live?

➢ Arid grasslands, scrub desert
➢ Alberta, Saskatchewan, south to Mexico

Did You Know...

◈ Sometimes called Horned Toads
◈ Females are bigger than males
◈ Body is wide, squat and flattened
◈ Back, sides and upper legs are covered with small spines, and the head has short, sharp spines projecting backwards
◈ Can change colour to match rock or sand habitat; nearly invisible if motionless
◈ Most abundant along south facing ravines
◈ Active during midday, and burrow into soil at night
◈ Rely on **camouflage** rather than speed for defense
◈ Flatten and tilt their bodies to catch the slanting rays of the sun
◈ Preferred diet is ants, but also eat insects, snails and small snakes

Special Concern
Loss of habitat
Agricultural
development

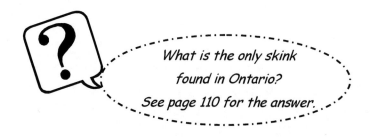

What is the only skink found in Ontario?
See page 110 for the answer.

Anguid Lizard Family
Anguidae

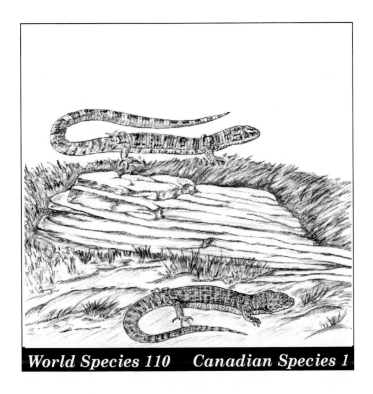

World Species 110   Canadian Species 1

Family Range
This widespread family is found in The Americas, Europe, Asia and Indo-China.

Characteristics
These lizards all have long, slender bodies with smooth, shiny scales. Lots of bony armor in the skin and bony plated scales on the underside means they have very stiff bodies. There is a fold or groove of softer scales that runs along their sides. This groove allows for expansion of the body for breathing, eating and egg carrying. They are sometimes referred to as *lateral fold lizards*. These short-limbed animals come in a variety of colours, but those in northern climates are generally darker, for increased heat absorption. They have a long tongue with a forked tip, and sharp crushing teeth. Most live on the ground. A few species live in trees, and have **prehensile** tails. They are solitary, secretive and slow moving animals.

Reproduction
Most species are egg-layers, and may guard the **clutch** until the eggs hatch. Others retain the eggs within their bodies and give birth to live young. There can be up to 26 babies in a litter.

Northern Alligator Lizard Lézard-alligator boreal
Elgaria caerulea

The largest lizards in Canada, these animals prefer cooler temperatures and are able to survive at higher elevations. This adaptation probably accounts for their presence in Canada, although they only live in the extreme southern portion.

Size 22-30 cm

Colour
Olive, greenish or bluish black, with indistinct blotches or spots

Reproduction
2-15 live young born
after 7-10 weeks

Where do they live?

➢ Cool moist forest, dry woodland
➢ British Columbia, south to California

Did You Know...

◆ Tail is up to half the body length, and **fragile**

◆ Juveniles have a broad, light coloured stripe down the back

◆ **Courtship** ritual involves neck biting

◆ Active at different times of day in different habitats

◆ Usually found under rotten logs, rocks or loose bark

◆ Exceptionally wary, taking cover at the first sign of danger

◆ Individuals with shorter tails have slower sprint speeds

◆ Are **carnivorous**, eating insects, small mammals, reptiles

◆ In the same family as legless lizards, or slowworms

◆ Time of mating varies in different latitudes

◆ Live in cool, moist forests up to 3,200 metres

◆ Known lifespan up to eight years

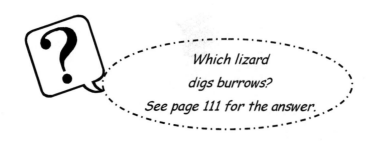

Which lizard digs burrows? See page 111 for the answer.

Skink Family
Scincidae

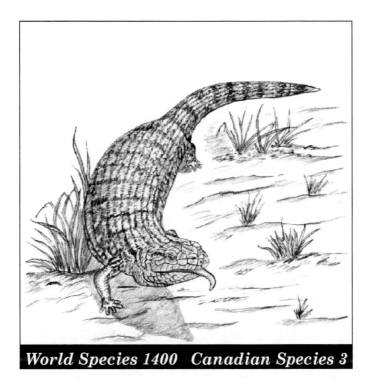

World Species 1400   Canadian Species 3

Family Range
Skinks are found in all tropical and **temperate regions** of the world. They are also widely distributed on oceanic islands.

Characteristics
While they have the long, skinny bodies of the rest of the lizard family, skinks have smooth scales that give them a polished, glossy look. They have small, flattened heads with round eyes. Their tongue is short, wide, flat and thick. Most skinks have small legs, but those adapted to burrowing have even shorter ones. Burrowing species have a window in the lower eyelid that lets them see while the eye is closed, to keep out dirt. These are extremely active, quick animals that hunt insects during daylight hours.

Reproduction
All North American members of this family are egg-layers. Females guard the eggs until they hatch, but no parental care is given to the young. Some members of this family have been known to move their eggs to a more suitable location by carrying them in their mouth.

Five-lined Skink *Scinque pentaligne*
Eumeces fasciatus

These are the common Blue-tailed Skinks of eastern North America, and the only lizard found in Ontario. They inhabit stable sand dunes and gardens in the Great Lakes region of Canada, and can be found on rocky slopes and under logs.

Size 17-20 cm

Colour
Black or brown with blue tail, and five light stripes down back

Reproduction
10-18 eggs hatch
after 1-2 months

Where do they live?

➤ Moist woodlands, open forest
➤ Southern Ontario, south to Gulf Coast

Did You Know...

◆ Juveniles have very bright stripes, and a bright blue tail that fades as they age

◆ **Terrestrial**, and climb only to escape predators or sun themselves on low branches

◆ Males establish a **territory** in breeding season, and develop a bright orange chin and jaw during that period

◆ Track their prey with a keen sense of smell; favourite foods are ants and spiders

◆ Become active only when full sun reaches their **territory**

◆ May overwinter in small groups, and can be found 2.4 metres underground

◆ Female stays near the nest for a day or so after the eggs hatch, but no parental care is given to the young

◆ Known lifespan up to six years

Special Concern

Loss of habitat
Poaching for
the pet trade

Prairie Skink Scinque des prairies
Eumeces septentrionalis

The Canadian population of these skinks has been separated from the one in the USA, which extends in a narrow band down to the Gulf Coast. They are the only lizard in Manitoba, and are limited to an area along the Assiniboine River.

Size 13-20 cm

Colour
Brown with four light stripes down the back

Reproduction
5-18 eggs hatch after 3-4 months

Where do they live?

➢ Sandy riversides
➢ Manitoba, south to Texas

Did You Know...

◆ Breeding males have orange on the side of the head

◆ Young have a bright blue tail that fades as they age

◆ Tail is **fragile**

◆ May construct burrows with entrances that form shallow dugouts under rocks

◆ Active dawn and dusk; shelter under rocks or in burrows during the heat of the day

◆ Food is mashed with their strong jaws before swallowing

◆ Inhabit sandy areas always close to water

◆ **Hibernate** in groups

◆ Limited to sandy areas, where loose soil allows them to burrow

◆ Cannot reproduce until three years of age, and only lay one **clutch** per year

◆ Illegal to keep them as pets in Manitoba, or collect them from the wild

Special Concern
Loss of habitat
Urban development

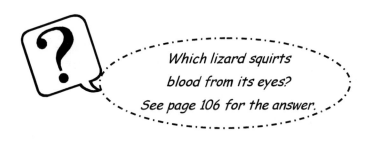

Which lizard squirts blood from its eyes? See page 106 for the answer.

Western Skink Scinque de l'ouest
Eumeces skiltonianus

These skinks have been found on islands off the coast of California. It is unknown how they reached the islands, but may have rafted out on mats of floating debris. Reptiles around the world have established island populations this way.

Size 16-20 cm

Colour
Brown or black, with four light stripes down the body

Reproduction
2-6 eggs hatch
after 2-3 months

Where do they live?

➢ Open woodlands, grasslands
➢ Southern British Columbia, south to California

Did You Know...

◆ Tail is longer than the body, and **fragile**
◆ Juveniles have a bright blue tail
◆ Breeding males have red lips and chin, and orange on the tip of the tail
◆ Scales may come off if the animal is roughly handled
◆ Extremely wary and agile
◆ Little is known of their life history
◆ Inhabit open bushy areas with abundant rocks
◆ Eat insects and their **larvae**, spiders and worms
◆ Active during the day but are rarely seen, spending most of their time under rocks or in rotten logs
◆ Females guard the eggs until they hatch
◆ Also found on Vancouver Island, BC
◆ Known lifespan up to six years

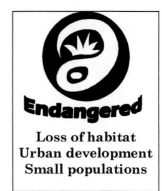

Endangered
Loss of habitat
Urban development
Small populations

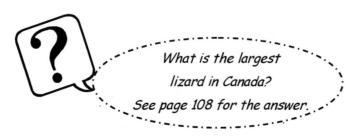

What is the largest lizard in Canada?
See page 108 for the answer.

snakes

SNAKES

These animals arouse more passion in people than any other. Their long, scaly body and lack of limbs, ears or eyelids are not what most people consider appealing. Their unblinking gaze is often thought to be evil or vicious. No other group of animals generates such strong emotions - from fascination to terror to hatred.

Habitat

Snakes are found on all continents except Antarctica, and are absent only from Ireland, Iceland and New Zealand. Their unique method of movement means they are equally at home on land or in water. They inhabit all major ecosystems except the polar areas.

Features

The body of the snake is a cleverly designed masterpiece. They have the same internal organs as other **vertebrates**, but theirs have been modified to fit a tubular body. Only boas and pythons have two lungs, while in all others the left lung is reduced or absent. The kidneys are placed one behind the other. Extra sections in the backbone have lengthened the body, and some snakes can have up to 400 vertebrae.

The two halves of their lower jaw are connected by elastic ligaments and move separately from each other. They also have highly moveable upper jaws. The ends of their ribs open, and the skin between the scales can be stretched for large items to pass though. To avoid choking, they extend a special breathing tube through the mouth to eat.

Their eyes are covered by a hard, transparent cap, which prevents injury when moving through vegetation. It is this eye cap which gives them their unblinking stare, and it is shed the same time as the skin. **Diurnal** snakes have round pupils, while those active at night have vertical pupils that shut to a tight slit, protecting the eyes from daylight.

Up to twenty sets of muscles on each side move the body. Forward motion is made by moving the enlarged scales, or **scutes**, on the belly. Each of these large scales is attached to two or more pairs of ribs. By moving them in groups, with some pushing forward while others push back, they are able to generate forward movement.

Some species subdue their prey with a poison called **venom**. It is located in special teeth called *fangs*, which function like a hypodermic syringe. Some species are

> Lacking external ears, snakes cannot hear airborne sounds. They can detect vibrations from the ground or water, which are sent through the body to the inner ear through bones connected to the lower jaw.

rear-fanged and must chew to bring the teeth into contact with their prey. Others have fixed front fangs, while some have moveable front fangs that are so long they must be folded back into the mouth when not in use.

Snake **venom** has helpful medical applications, and is the subject of a great deal of biochemical and pharmacological research. Compounds made from **venom** have been used to treat high blood pressure, and increase circulation. **Venomous** snakes bite several hundred thousand people around the world each year. If properly treated, less than 1% of these people will die. Snakes avoid contact with people, and most bites occur because they feel threatened, or because people seek contact with them.

Snakes only need to eat six to thirty meals a year, totaling 55-300% of their body mass. Some eat prey more than one and a half times their body weight. No single predator eats the remarkable range of prey taken by the snake family, from tiny ant eggs to 23 kilogram antelope. All species are **carnivorous**.

Family Life

Snakes do not have visual **courtship** displays like the lizards. During mating season, females emit a chemical scent, or *pheromone*. The male picks up this scent with his tongue, and follows her trail. He approaches the female slowly, rubs his chin on her back, then wraps his body around hers. This pheromone enables them to communicate with other members of their species.

Garter snakes are famous for their mating balls. From 30-100 males gather and coil around each female. The group becomes a squirming mass until the female is mated, then the mass breaks up. The males of some garter snakes insert a plug in the female after mating, so she cannot mate with others.

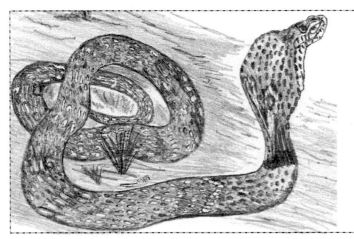

Like all snakes, the Indian Cobra is unable to hear airborne sounds. A snake-charmer really hypnotizes them with the movements of his flute, not the sound.

Spectacular Snakes !

The smallest snake in the world is the Thread Snake
of the Caribbean. At just 10 cm long, their body is
so thin they can enter the hole in a pencil where
the lead has been removed.

▼

The fastest snake in the world is the Black Mamba
of Africa. Speeds up to 19 km in short bursts
have been recorded.

▼

Peringuey's Adders of Africa flatten their body so
dew sits on it, then lick up the water and raise
their head to swallow.

▼

Possibly the most **venomous** species in the world
is the Australian Sea Snake; human fatalities are
rare because they live in the open ocean.

▼

A billion dollar drug to treat high blood pressure
was inspired from a component in the **venom** of
the South American Jararacas.

▼

African Sand Snakes polish their entire bodies
from special glands on their head.

▼

The largest snake on record is the South American
Anaconda, with one female measuring 227 kg
and 8.45 metres long.

▼

The Jumping Viper of Central America curls its body
into an 'S' shape and springs up to one metre in the air.

▼

The highest recorded elevation for any snake is the
Himalayan Pit Viper, found at 5,000 metres at
the foot of a glacier in India.

▼

Asian Burrowing Snakes have fringed lips.

▼

Australia has more venomous snakes than any other
country, but more people die from snakebite in
India than anywhere else in the world.

▲

Boa Family
Boidae

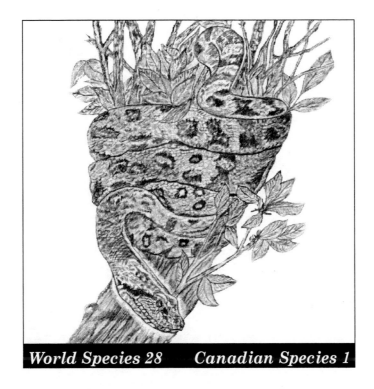

World Species 28   Canadian Species 1

Family Range

These are the giants of the snake world, and can reach over nine metres in length. They are found in The Americas, Africa, western Asia, India and the islands of the South Pacific. The greatest number of species are found in tropical or subtropical areas.

Characteristics

Boas have stout, muscular bodies with short tails. The scales on the back are smooth and sometimes **iridescent**. The larger belly scales form crosswise plates. These snakes are constrictors, wrapping loops of their body around their prey. Each time their victim breathes, the snake tightens their grip, to the point where breathing finally becomes impossible. Most species live on the ground, or spend much of their time in the trees. Some of the smaller species, including the one found in Canada, are burrowers, and prefer to live in areas with loose or sandy soil for easier digging.

Reproduction

Members of this family all give birth to live young in rock dens, or cavities made of tree roots.

Rubber Boa Boa caoutehouc
Charina bottae

Like many Canadian reptiles, these boas give birth to live young, sometimes only every two or three years. They reproduce in late summer, and may be unable to eat enough before entering **hibernation** *to reproduce the following summer.*

Size 35-83 cm

Colour
Olive, reddish brown,
tan or dark brown

Reproduction
2-8 live young born
in late summer

Where do they live?

➤ Damp woodlands, wet meadows
➤ Southern British Columbia, south to California

Did You Know...

◈ Sometimes called the Two-headed Snake, as the broad snout and blunt tail look similar

◈ Like all boas, they have traces of hind limbs

◈ Smooth scales and wrinkled skin give them a rubbery appearance

◈ Found up to 2,800 metres in damp woodlands and grassy areas

◈ A burrowing species that require habitat with loose soil

◈ **Nocturnal**; retreat under rocks, logs, or into burrows during the day

◈ Good swimmers and climbers; their **prehensile** tail helps them grip shrubs and small trees

◈ Very tame species; method of defence is to curl into a tight ball with the head hidden and the tail exposed

◈ Prey is killed by **constriction**; main prey species is young mice still in the nest

◈ Newborn snakes are around 17 centimetres long

◈ Known lifespan up to 11 years

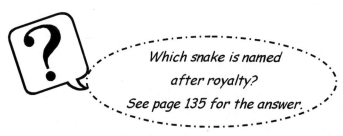

Which snake is named after royalty?
See page 135 for the answer.

Viper Family
Viperidae

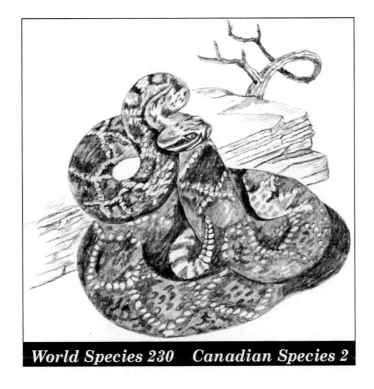

World Species 230   Canadian Species 2

Family Range
Vipers are found in The Americas, Europe, Africa, Asia and Indo-China. Two heat sensitive pits located on the sides of the head enable them to locate warm-blooded prey, even at night. Another name for these animals is Pit Vipers.

Characteristics
These snakes all have large, triangular shaped heads, which are flattened above, and wider than their body. They subdue their prey by injecting **venom**, and are able to regulate the amount secreted. A dark band behind each eye protects the poison in the head glands from ultra-violet radiation. Their **venom** acts on the victim's blood tissue, breaking down the red blood cells and causing internal bleeding. Two hollow, curved fangs are located near the front of the mouth. They are folded back along the jaw, and swung forward only to strike. These fangs are so important to the snake that new ones grow in before the old ones are shed.

Reproduction
The Canadian members of the Viper family all give birth to live young, and stay with them for a few days after hatching.

Rattlesnakes

The North American members of the Viper family are the rattlesnakes. Their tail has a series of connected, flattened segments which rub together and produce a buzzing sound when shaken. Newborn rattlers have just a button on their tail, with more segments being added each time the skin is shed, usually two to four times a year. When moving, rattlers lift their tail off the ground to protect the rattle, which is their main method of defense. They do not always rattle before striking. Having no external ears, these snakes cannot hear the sound of their own rattle. Newly hatched rattlers have **venom** as **toxic** as that of the adults, and rattlesnakes are not immune to their own poison.

<u>These snakes are not aggressive. They do not strike people except in self-defence, but may do a false strike to scare if they feel threatened.</u>

*Members of the Viper family have moveable front fangs. These hollow fangs swing forward to the front of the mouth when needed, and inject **venom** into their prey.*

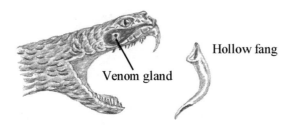

Venom gland

Hollow fang

Massassauga Rattlesnake Massasauga
Sisturnus catenatus

Their name means "great river mouth" in Chippewa, and probably refers to their preferred habitat. Unlike the grassland dwellers, these snakes are found near bogs, swamps and marshes. They are more **aquatic** *than other rattlers.*

Size 51-76 cm

Colour
Tan, grayish, yellowish brown, with dark blotches on back and sides

Reproduction
Up to 20 live young are born in late summer

Where do they live?

➢ Bogs, swamps, dry woodland
➢ South western Ontario, south to Mexico

Did You Know...

◆ Also called Swamp Rattlesnake and Little Gray Rattlesnake
◆ Canada's smallest rattlesnake, reaching a maximum of 76 cm
◆ When coiled, they will fit onto a plate
◆ **Venom** is about five times as deadly as that of the Western Diamondback in the USA, but is produced in smaller quantities
◆ Active at dusk, dawn and night in the summer, but may be seen basking on mild days
◆ Canadian range is thought to be limited to an area around Georgian Bay, plus a few other small areas in Ontario
◆ Mild mannered, preferring to retreat rather than attack
◆ Will eat dead and decaying food, but main prey species is mice
◆ Newborn snakelets are 20 cm long
◆ Known lifespan up to 17 years

Threatened
Loss of habitat Persecution by humans

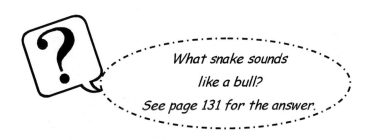

What snake sounds like a bull?
See page 131 for the answer.

Western Rattlesnake Crotale de l'ouest
Crotalus viridis

The western counterpart of the smaller eastern species, these animals are found in grasslands and open areas of the west. Their colour means they blend in well with the grassland vegetation. Much of their distribution is in sparcely settled areas.

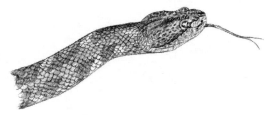

Size 40-162 cm

Colour
Greenish or yellowish brown
with white bordered dark blotches

Reproduction
Up to 20 live young are
born in late summer

Where do they live?

➢ Grasslands, sand dunes
➢ Southern British Columbia, Alberta, Saskatchewan, south to Mexico

Did You Know...

◈ Maximum length 1.6 metres but are generally smaller

◈ Large numbers overwinter together in the same den

◈ Active dawn, dusk and night

◈ Shelter in abandoned mammal burrows, under rocks or in cavities

◈ Do not share a burrow with prairie dogs as once believed, but prey on these animals

◈ Rattle their tails at 20-100 times per second; the warmer the snake, the faster the rattle

◈ Eat small, crop destroying mammals such as mice and rats

◈ Mate late summer or fall; female gives birth the following spring

◈ Newborns are around 21 centimetres at birth; female stays near them for a few days after hatching

◈ Females do not reproduce until six to eight years of age, and give birth every two or more years

◈ Known lifespan up to 19 years

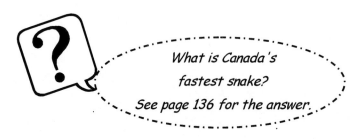

What is Canada's fastest snake?
See page 136 for the answer.

Harmless Snake Family
Colubridae

World Species 1700 Canadian Species 21

Family Range

This is the largest snake family, containing more than three quarters of the world's snake species. They are found on all continents except Antarctica, and range from the Arctic Circle in the north to the southern tip of Africa.

Characteristics

Due to the size of this family, there is a large variety of physical characteristics. Generally, the head is as wide or just slightly wider than the neck. Scales on the back and sides are regularly arranged, and those on the belly are as wide as the body. Eyes are either round or vertical, depending on their **diurnal** or **nocturnal** lifestyles. In some species, there are small, backward facing teeth to hold slippery, struggling prey. These snakes have no **venom**, but many species vibrate their tail in dry vegetation to imitate the sound made by rattlesnakes. They will also exude a foul smelling scent from their **anal glands** to deter predators.

Reproduction

Both live bearers and egg layers are found in this family.

Black Rat Snake Couleuvre obscure
Elaphe obsoleta

Rat snakes are large, powerful constrictors. They are sometimes called Pilot Black Snakes, from the belief that they lead other snakes to safety or winter dens. They are also called Highland Black Snakes because of their fondness for open country.

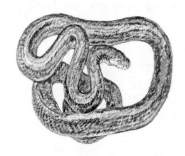

Size 86-256 cm

Colour
Black, red, orange, yellow, brown or gray, with dark stripes

Reproduction
Up to 30 eggs hatch after 1-2 months

Where do they live?

➢ Hardwood forest, canyons, fields
➢ Southern Ontario, south to Mexico

Did You Know...

◈ Also called Chicken Snake
◈ Canada's largest snake, up to 2.5 metres long
◈ Markings may be striped, blotched or not present at all
◈ Species has three different colour patterns; population in Canada is black, with a white chin and throat
◈ Semi-**arboreal**, feeding on young birds, eggs, small mammals
◈ Vibrate their tail in dry vegetation as a warning; will strike if cornered but their bite is harmless
◈ Skillful climber and can often be found in trees
◈ Frequently share winter dens with rattlesnakes in the USA
◈ Reproduce only every other year
◈ Have been observed to guard their eggs in captivity
◈ Known lifespan up to 25 years

Threatened
Loss of habitat
Urban development
Persecution

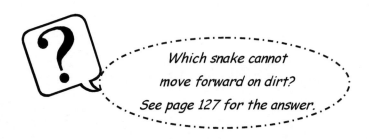

Which snake cannot move forward on dirt? See page 127 for the answer.

124

Brown Snake Couleuvre brune
Storeria dekayi

These small snakes can be found living in parks, golf courses, gardens and vacant lots. They are welcome visitors to the gardener, as 60% of their diet consists of slugs. Other habitats include fresh and saltwater marshes and moist woodlands.

Size 25-52 cm

Colour
Gray, yellowish or reddish brown, with back stripe and two rows of small spots

Reproduction
Up to 30 live young born in late summer

Where do they live?

➢ Moist woodland, marshes
➢ South western Ontario, Quebec, south to Central America

Did You Know...

◈ Also called Dekay's Snake, after a New York naturalist

◈ Juveniles are black or gray with a light coloured ring around the neck

◈ Belly is pinkish white

◈ Always found near water; require some dampness in their habitat, and avoid dry areas

◈ If threatened, they flatten their bodies to appear larger

◈ Usually **diurnal**, but may be active at night in very warm weather

◈ Spend most of their time underground, or under rocks or logs

◈ Newborns are 8-11 centimetres at birth

◈ Large numbers **hibernate** together, and many are killed on roads as they **migrate** to and from their den

◈ Eat earthworms, slugs and snails

◈ Known lifespan up to seven years

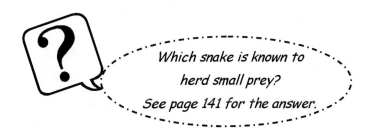

Which snake is known to herd small prey? See page 141 for the answer.

Eastern Fox Snake Couleuvre fauve de l'est
Elaphe gloydi

This snake was once considered a subspecies of the Fox Snake, which is found throughout eastern and central USA. The species has recently been split into two, the Eastern and Western Fox Snakes. The Western Fox Snake is not found in Canada.

Size 86-179 cm

Colour
Yellow to brown, with
dark blotches down the back

Reproduction
15-20 eggs hatch
after 1-2 months

Where do they live?

➢ Great Lakes shoreline
➢ South western Ontario, south to Missouri

Did You Know...

◆ Sometimes called Hardwood Rattler, for their habit of vibrating the tail in vegetation
◆ Belly is yellow and has a black checkerboard pattern
◆ One of Canada's largest snakes, they can grow to 1.8 metres
◆ Entire population is found in the Great Lakes Region of North America; most of their range is in Canada
◆ Secrete a strong smelling liquid similar to the smell of a fox
◆ Excellent climbers and have been seen ten metres up in trees
◆ Have been seen swimming in the cold waters of Georgian Bay
◆ Always found near water
◆ Feed mainly on rodents, with prey killed by **constriction**
◆ **Hibernate** in groups with other snake species
◆ Newborn snakelets are 25-30 centimetres long
◆ Known lifespan up to 17 years

Threatened
Loss of habitat
Urban development
Persecution

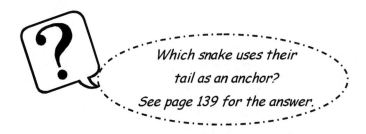

Which snake uses their tail as an anchor?
See page 139 for the answer.

Garter Snakes

Canada has six species of garter snake. These small snakes are found from Vancouver Island to the Maritimes, and are absent only from Newfoundland. They live in a wide variety of habitats.

All species have a common defense mechanism of releasing a foul smelling scent from their **anal glands**. *They may bite if handled, but are harmless. Garter snakes are* **diurnal**, *and may often be seen basking during the early morning hours.*

Size
45-97 cm

Colour
Olive brown to black, with yellow, orange or red stripes down the body

Reproduction
3-85 live young are born in mid-summer

Where do they live?

➢ Wet meadows, deciduous forest
➢ See details below

Butler's Garter Snake Couleuvre à petite tête
Thamnophis butleri

Range: Sw Ontario, south to Ohio

❖ Similar to the Common Garter and Eastern Ribbon Snake
❖ Smallest garter snake in Ontario
❖ Live in open, wetland edges
❖ A gentle, non-aggressive snake
❖ Move swiftly through grass, but if placed on dirt or frightened, they move in a side-winding motion with little forward movement
❖ **Prehensile** tail grips vegetation when escaping predators
❖ Home range size is around 270 square metres
❖ Eat mainly earthworms
❖ Canadian range makes up the majority of their total range

Threatened
Loss of habitat
Draining wetlands
Road mortality

➡

Common (Red-sided) Garter Snake Couleuvre rayée
Thamnophis sirtalis

Range: NWT, British Columbia to the Maritimes, south through USA

◆ **Melanistic** forms with white chins have been found in Ontario and Nova Scotia
◆ Most abundant and widespread snake in Canada
◆ Widest range of any North American snake; found as far north as Ft. Smith, NWT
◆ Can tolerate cool weather, and may be active year round in the southern part of their range
◆ Up to 8,000 individuals may occupy some winter dens
◆ Travel many kilometres from winter den to summer feeding areas
◆ Frequently seen in moist vegetation
◆ Eat frogs, toads, salamanders, worms, mice, small fish
◆ Often form mating balls, with up to 100 males intertwined around a single female
◆ Young remain together for a few weeks after hatching
◆ Known lifespan up to 14 years

Eastern Ribbon Snake Couleuvre mince
Thamnophis sauritus

Range: Southern Ontario, Nova Scotia, south to Florida

◆ More slender and streamlined than other garter snakes
◆ Have a very long tail
◆ Semi-**aquatic**, and always live in low, wet places
◆ May be found climbing or basking in low bushes next to water
◆ Take to water if pursued, gliding across the surface
◆ May become temporarily inactive during very dry summers
◆ Timid and nervous species
◆ Isolated population in Nova Scotia is listed as endangered
◆ Preferred food is amphibians, and do not eat earthworms
◆ Known lifespan up to four years

Special Concern

**Loss of habitat
Isolated
populations**

→

Northwestern Garter Snake Couleuvre du nord-ouest
Thamnophis ordinoides

Range: Vancouver Island, south western British Columbia, south to California

◆ Colour is variable, and both white and black specimens
   are fairly common
◆ Eat mainly slugs and earthworms
◆ Rarely enter water
◆ Common species on Vancouver Island and the lower
   mainland of British Columbia
◆ Found in open grassy area and pastures
◆ Most active on sunny days
◆ Known lifespan up to 15 years

Plains Garter Snake Couleuvre des plaines
Thamnophis radix

Range: Southern Alberta, Saskatchewan and Manitoba, south to New Mexico

◆ Most colourful garter snake; have bright yellow or orange stripes and a
   checkerboard pattern on the back
◆ A common species throughout their range
◆ Found in wet meadows and open prairies
◆ Hunt along the edge of water bodies
◆ Favorite prey species is the Northern Leopard Frog,
   which is rapidly disappearing
◆ May be seen basking on warm days
◆ **Hibernate** in mammal burrows or rock piles
◆ Up to 92 young have been born in a single litter
◆ Males seek out a female by following her scent trail, and learn the direction by
   sensing concentrations on opposite sides of grass blades
◆ Known lifespan up to seven years

→

Western Terrestrial Garter Snake Couleuvre de l'ouest
Thamnopis elegans

Range: British Columbia, Alberta, Saskatchewan, south to Mexico

❖ Also called Wandering Garter Snake
❖ Differ from other garter snakes with eight scales on their upper lip
❖ Adults can be up to one metre in length
❖ Often take to water if disturbed
❖ May be seen basking during the morning hours
❖ Hunt in tidal pools for fish left behind at low tide
❖ Eat soft-bodied **invertebrates** such as slugs and earthworms
❖ Inhabit open forest and grassy areas always near water
❖ Found from sea level to 3,200 metres
❖ Prey captured in water and on land
❖ Known lifespan up to nine years

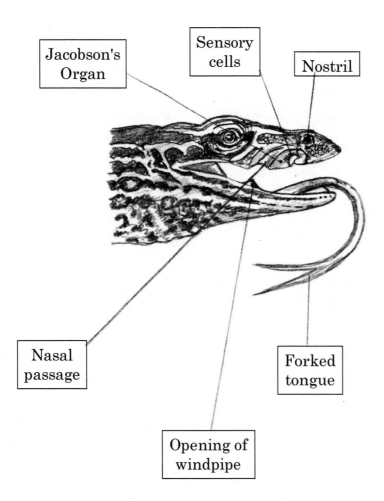

Jacobson's Organ

Sensory cells

Nostril

Nasal passage

Forked tongue

Opening of windpipe

Gopher (Bull) Snake Couleuvre à nez mince
Pituphis melanoleucus

Living in farming and ranching areas, these are Canada's most economically beneficial snakes. An estimate has been made that the rodents eaten by these snakes could cause over four hundred million dollars in damage annually to the grain crop.

Size 1.2-2 m

Colour
Brown, tan, yellowish, with dark blotches on back and sides

Reproduction
Up to 25 eggs hatch
after 60-80 days

Where do they live?

➤ Dry woodlands, grasslands
➤ Southern British Columbia, Alberta, Saskatchewan, south to Mexico

Did You Know...

◆ Also called Pine Snake, or Pacific Gopher Snake
◆ Large, powerfully built snakes; may reach two metres
◆ Small head is flattened; pointed outline helps them see forward in mammal burrows
◆ Vibrate tail in vegetation and are often killed as rattlesnakes
◆ Coil and hiss explosively like the snort of a bull; hissing sound can be heard 15 metres away
◆ Share communal winter dens with rattlesnakes
◆ Usually **diurnal**, but may be active at night in hot weather
◆ Defense behaviour of hissing, flattening their head, vibrating their tail and lunging at the intruder
◆ One snake 1.5 metres long had 25 mice in its stomach
◆ Female coils around the eggs and guards them until they hatch
◆ Unknown if any still live in British Columbia
◆ Known lifespan up to 22 years

Hognose Snakes

Hognose Snakes are heavy bodied, with flattened heads and modified scales on the nose that give them an up-turned look. They are also known as Puff Adders or Spreading Adders for their defensive tactic of spreading their neck, inflating their body and hissing loudly before striking. People often assume they are dangerous, and kill them on sight.

Size
Eastern 50-115 cm
Western 40-89 cm

Colour
Tan, yellowish, brown, gray or reddish with dark blotches

Reproduction
20-60 eggs hatch after 7-9 weeks

Where do they live?

➤ Fields, bushy areas, meadows
➤ See below for details

Eastern Hognose Snake
Couleuvre à nez plat
Heterodon platirhinos

Range: Southern Ontario, south to Florida

Threatened

Western Hognose Snake
Couleuvre à nez retroussé
Heterodon nasicus

Range: Southern Alberta, Saskatchewan, Manitoba, south to Mexico

◈ **Melanistic** individuals have been found in eastern Canada
◈ Sense of smell enables them to find buried toads, lizards or eggs
◈ Have an additional defence posture of rolling on their backs with their mouth open and 'playing dead'; if turned upright they flip again
◈ Always strike with their mouth closed; not known to bite
◈ Was once believed their breath was poisonous
◈ Feed largely on toads; have enlarged teeth on upper jaw to puncture the toad when they inflate their bodies
◈ Can burrow into loose soil using their snout
◈ Prey is grabbed and swallowed, not killed by **constriction**
◈ Known lifespan up to 19 years

Milk Snake Couleuvre tachetée
Lampropetis triangulum

Milk Snakes were named from a wrong idea. Like most snakes, they frequent barns in search of mice, and it was once thought they sucked the milk from cows. Although blamed for low milk production, with their sharp teeth and bite this is impossible.

Size   35-199 cm

Colour
Gray or tan, with 'v' or 'y' shaped patch on neck and dark blotches

Reproduction
Up to 17 eggs hatch after 2-3 months

Where do they live?

➤ Forest, meadows, grasslands
➤ Southern Ontario, Quebec, south to Venezuela

Did You Know...

◆ Blotches on the body may be red, orange, yellow or black
◆ Adult size varies geographically, with North American snakes smaller than those in the tropics
◆ Record length 1.3 metres, but most are 0.6 to 0.9 metres
◆ Have one of the largest ranges of any North American snake
◆ Secretive and not usually seen except at night
◆ More than 70% of their diet is mice; also eat birds, lizards and a variety of snake species
◆ Prey is killed by **constriction**
◆ Vibrate their tail in vegetation if cornered, and often killed as a rattlesnake
◆ Known lifespan up to 21 years

Special Concern

Road mortality
Persecution
Small populations

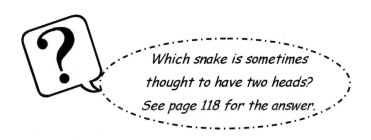

Which snake is sometimes thought to have two heads? See page 118 for the answer.

Night Snake Couleuvre nocturne
Hypsigiena torquata

*Canada's only rear-fanged snake, the bite of the
Night Snake is in no way dangerous to humans.
Enlarged teeth located far in the back of the upper
jaw secrete a mildly **toxic** saliva that subdues
their small rodent, bird or insect prey.*

Size 30-66 cm

Colour
Tan, yellowish or gray,
with dark blotches and bars

Reproduction
4-6 eggs hatch
after 4-5 weeks

Where do they live?

➢ Grasslands, bushy desert
➢ Southern British Columbia, south
to Costa Rica

Did You Know...

◈ Also called Desert Night Snake
◈ Have large, dark blotches on each side of the neck
◈ One of the rarest snakes in Canada, but widespread in the
western USA and Central America
◈ Little is known of their life history
◈ Have a threat display of raising their head, weaving, hissing
and flattening their neck
◈ **Nocturnal** and have vertical eye pupils like a cat
◈ Known to eat juvenile rattlesnakes; young feed on insects
◈ Only discovered in Canada in 1980
◈ British Columbia is the northern tip of their range
◈ Known lifespan up to nine years

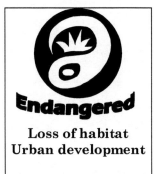

Endangered
Loss of habitat
Urban development

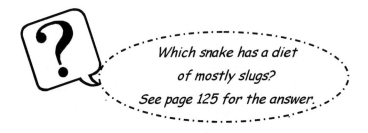

*Which snake has a diet
of mostly slugs?*
See page 125 for the answer.

Queen Snake Couleuvre royale
Regina septemvittata

Crayfish make up the specialized diet of these snakes. When newborn Queen Snakes are offered several different odours on cotton swabs, they attack that of the crayfish, ignoring all others. In turn, large crayfish may prey upon young snakes.

Size 40-93 cm

Colour
Tan, olive or brown,
with stripes along the body

Reproduction
Up to 20 live young
are born mid-summer

Did You Know...

◈ Can grow to almost one metre long

◈ The only snake with a striped underside

◈ Active day or night

◈ Highly **aquatic**, and rest on branches overhanging water bodies

◈ Seldom found more than three metres from water

◈ Inhabit streams and slow rivers with rocky bottoms

◈ Excellent swimmers and divers

◈ Very swift snakes, almost impossible to catch

◈ Prefer freshly moulted crayfish

◈ **Hibernate** in large groups

◈ Newborn snakelets are 19-23 cm at birth

◈ Highly susceptible to mercury poisoning in water

◈ Known lifespan up to 19 years

Where do they live?

➢ River shorelines, marshes
➢ South western Ontario, south to Florida

Threatened
Loss of habitat
Urban development
Water pollution

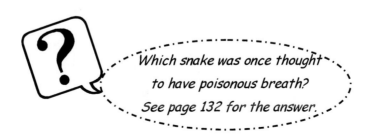

Which snake was once thought to have poisonous breath?

See page 132 for the answer.

Racer Couleuvre agile
Coluber constrictor

As their name suggests, these large, slender snakes are agile and fast moving. They can glide over the tops of bushes almost as quickly as on the ground, and have been recorded at speeds of nearly seven kilometres an hour on open ground.

Size 86-195 cm

Colour
Black, blue, yellowish,
dark brown or olive

Reproduction
9-15 eggs hatch
after 3-4 months

Where do they live?

➢ Grasslands, open woodlands
➢ British Columbia, Saskatchewan, Ontario, south to Mexico

Did You Know...

◈ May reach 1.9 metres, but are usually smaller

◈ Have a long, whip-like tail

◈ Three separate subspecies in Canada, each with different colouring

◈ Active during the day

◈ **Migrate** three to five kilometres to and from winter den sites

◈ Often **bask** in the branches of shrubs, and lie on roads in cool weather to absorb heat

◈ Head is held up off the ground when searching for prey

◈ May vibrate tail in dead vegetation if threatened

◈ Prey may be held down by a loop of the body

◈ **Hibernate** in groups, sometimes with rattlesnakes

◈ Newborn snakelets are 20-33 centimetres at birth

◈ Blue Racer (ON) listed as endangered, and Yellow-bellied Racer (SK) listed as Special Concern

◈ Known lifespan up to 15 years

Endangered

**Loss of habitat
Road mortality
Isolated population**

Red-bellied Snake Couleuvre à ventre rouge
Storeria occipitomaculata

These tiny little snakes are very sedentary, and may never move more than 500 metres from their den site in wooded areas near bogs and swamps. They make use of the same wintering den each year.

Size 20-40 cm

Colour
Brown, gray or black,
with stripes down the body

Reproduction
Up to 20 live young
born mid-summer

Where do they live?

➤ Open woodlands, fields
➤ South eastern Saskatchewan to the Maritimes, south to Texas

Did You Know...

◈ Also known as Worm Snake and Spot-necked Snake
◈ Underside is bright orange, red or yellow
◈ When startled or threatened, they curl their upper lip and show their teeth
◈ Hide under boards, rocks or logs during the day
◈ Eat slugs, snails, earthworms and insects
◈ Teeth curve inward to hold soft, slimy prey
◈ May climb trees or shrubs
◈ Active during the day in spring and fall, and at twilight or night in the summer
◈ Sexually mature in two years
◈ Newborn snakelets are 7-10 centimetres at birth
◈ Valuable allies to blueberry farmers, as they prey on the slugs that damage the crop
◈ Large numbers are killed on roads as they **migrate** to and from the den
◈ Known lifespan up to four years

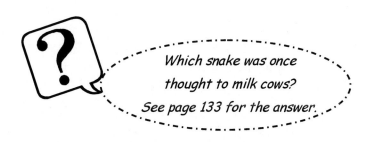

Which snake was once thought to milk cows?
See page 133 for the answer.

Ringneck Snake Couleuvre à collier
Diadophis punctatus

If threatened, Ringnecks with red bellies coil their tail tightly and lift it to display their brightly coloured underside. Bright colours in nature are often a sign the animal is poisonous, but these gentle, secretive snakes are harmless.

Size 25-76 cm

Colour
Gray, greenish, brown or black, with neck ring of yellow, cream or red

Reproduction
Up to 10 eggs hatch
after 7-8 weeks

Where do they live?

➤ Grasslands, open forest
➤ Southern Ontario to the Maritimes, south to Florida

Did You Know...

◈ Underside of the body is bright red or yellow
◈ Very gentle and secretive species
◈ Usually found under rocks, logs or bark and seldom seen basking
◈ Rarely bite, but emit a foul smelling secretion from the **anal glands** if picked up
◈ Retreat underground for part of the summer
◈ Partially constrict prey
◈ Feed mostly on Redback Salamanders
◈ **Nocturnal**, and rarely seen before dusk
◈ Elongated eggs are white with yellow ends, and increase in size after being laid
◈ Known lifespan up to six years

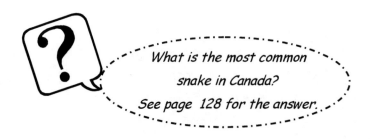

What is the most common snake in Canada? See page 128 for the answer.

Sharptail Snake Couleuvre à queue fine
Contia tenuis

Aptly named animals, these small snakes have a cone-shaped tail that ends with a pointed scale. It is thought they use it as an anchor, bracing themselves with it while capturing prey, but very little is known of their life history.

Size 25-48 cm

Colour
Brown, yellowish, gray
or reddish brown

Reproduction
2-8 eggs hatch
after 3-4 months

Where do they live?

➤ Open forest, pastures, meadows
➤ South western British Columbia, south to California

Did You Know...

◆ Have long, needle like teeth for gripping and eating slippery prey
◆ Belly has alternating black and white crossbars
◆ Smallest snake in British Columbia
◆ Are most active in the rainy season, and retreat underground during long, dry periods
◆ Have been found at a depth of 2.5 metres underground
◆ Able to adapt to lower temperatures than other snakes
◆ **Nocturnal** and rarely seen out in the open
◆ Diet is mainly slugs
◆ Found only on Vancouver Island, and other Gulf Islands
◆ Illegal to keep them as pets in British Columbia
◆ Threatened by urban development of their coastal habitat

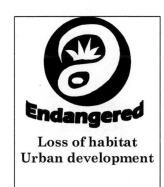

Endangered

**Loss of habitat
Urban development**

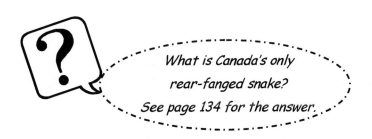

*What is Canada's only rear-fanged snake?
See page 134 for the answer.*

Smooth Green Snake Couleuvre verte
Opheodrys vernalis

Bright, satiny green with no markings, these are Canada's most beautiful snakes. They can be found in shrubs or vines, where they blend in. When clinging to a branch, the forward part of their body sways, mimicking greenery in a breeze.

Size 35-66 cm

Colour
Bright grass green

Reproduction
3-10 eggs hatch
after 1-2 weeks

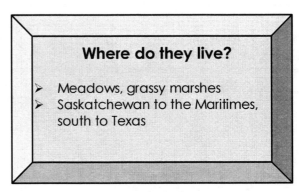

Where do they live?

➤ Meadows, grassy marshes
➤ Saskatchewan to the Maritimes, south to Texas

Did You Know...

◈ Also called Grass Snake or Green Snake
◈ Large numbers may overwinter together
◈ Found in grassy clearings and a variety of moist habitats
◈ Usually live on the ground, but are excellent climbers
◈ Eat insects, spiders, slugs and snails
◈ Active during the day
◈ Do not bite when handled, but will sometimes make a false strike
◈ Sexually mature in their second year
◈ **Hibernate** underground
◈ Female carries the eggs inside her body for a brief period
◈ Eggs are deposited under boards or flat stones that are warmed by the sun, keeping the **incubation** temperature up
◈ Known lifespan up to six years

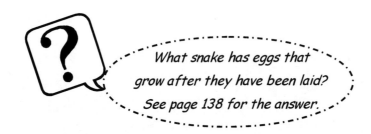

What snake has eggs that grow after they have been laid?
See page 138 for the answer.

Water Snake Couleuvre d'eau
Nerodia sipedon

As their name suggests, these snakes are highly **aquatic**. *They live in almost any permanent water body in their range. These harmless snakes are often thought to be deadly Water Moccasins, which have never lived in Canada, and killed on sight.*

Size 55-134 cm

Colour
Brown, gray, black or reddish, with dark crossbands on the neck

Reproduction
15-30 live young
born late summer

Where do they live?

➢ Clear streams, rivers, lakes
➢ Southern Ontario and Quebec, south to Oklahoma

Did You Know...

◆ One subspecies, the Lake Erie Water Snake, is endangered
◆ Saliva has an anti-coagulant quality, so wounds from their bite bleed profusely
◆ Scales are shiny on the head, but dull on the body
◆ Can be seen basking in groups on rocky shorelines, in shrubs or branches overhanging water
◆ Can be found three metres below the water surface and several kilometres from shore in the water
◆ **Hibernate** away from the water in rock piles
◆ Small prey is swallowed head first; large fish are eaten on shore
◆ Eat dead and diseased fish, and destructive lamprey eels
◆ Known to herd **tadpoles** or small fish toward shore with their bodies, making them easier to catch
◆ Known lifespan up to nine years

Endangered
Loss of habitat
Persecution
Water pollution

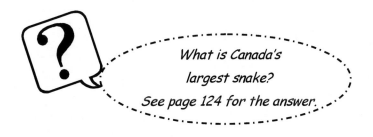

What is Canada's largest snake? See page 124 for the answer.

Conservation

Endangered

Loss of habitat
Persecution
Urban development
Road mortality
Poaching for pets
Chemicals
Water pollution
Introduced fish

Extirpated Species—Understanding Conservation Terms

It has been estimated that Canada is home to 70,000 wild species. In a study done by the federal and provincial governments in 2000, it was found that around 10% of our wild species either are at risk, or may be at risk in the near future. Some species are in more danger than others—40% of our reptiles and amphibians are either *endangered, threatened,* or listed as *special concern*. Some are already gone, and classified as *extirpated* from Canada. Other species are listed as *not at risk*, or *data deficient*.

These terms are used to identify the status of wild animals. The Committee on the Status of Endangered Wildlife in Canada (COSEWIC), compiles a list of all our wild species that need attention. How close each species is to extinction is shown by the following listings.

Extinct	No longer exist anywhere in the world
Extirpated	No longer exist in Canada, but may be found elsewhere
Endangered	At a high risk of extinction, or extirpation
Threatened	Likely to become endangered if present conditions continue
Special Concern	Existence is very vulnerable to human or natural changes
Not At Risk	Have been studied and found to be not at risk
Data Deficient	Not enough known about how safe the species is

Five species are already listed as Extirpated from Canada:

Timber Rattlesnake	Extirpated since 1941
Pacific Pond Turtle	Extirpated since 1959
Pygmy Short-horned Lizard	Extirpated since 1898
Pacific Gopher Snake	Extirpated since 1950
Eastern Tiger Salamander	Extirpated since 1915

Of our 70,000 species, we know the status of less than 1% of them. There are at least 600 other species that COSEWIC are concerned about, but without more money and time to investigate them, their status remains unknown.

For more details, please see the following web pages:

COSEWIC http://www.cosewic.gc.ca

Species At Risk http://www.speciesatrisk.gc.ca

Threats and Solutions

Amphibians and reptiles make up an important component of Canadian biodiversity. They occupy all habitats from marine to prairie to forest. A total of 16 amphibians and 26 reptiles have been designated as Endangered, Threatened or Special Concern by the Committee on the Status of Endangered Wildlife in Canada (COSEWIC).

These animals face a number of serious threats. Here is a list of those dangers, and things that should be done to protect these animals.

Habitat Loss and Fragmentation—the greatest threat of all
- Protect and save the wetlands
- Identify areas that have lots of reptiles and amphibians
- Locate and protect communal dens

Human Persecution
- Educate people on the benefits these animals provide to mankind, and why they shouldn't be killed on sight

Traffic Mortality
- Build roadside barriers in areas used by large numbers of these animals

Chemical Contaminants
- Reduce agricultural and chemical runoff into waterways such as lakes and rivers
- Reduce use of pesticides

Increased Ultraviolet Radiation
- Make sure lots of plants-trees, shrubs, grasses-remain for their shelter

Lack of Biological Knowledge
- Study them in the wild to see what they need to survive
- Fund this type of conservation research

Illegal Collection for the Pet Trade
- Educate people as to why they shouldn't pick up wild animals
- Enforce the laws that protect the animals
- Work with responsible members of the pet trade to stop this practice

Introduction of Infectious Diseases
- Ban the selling of frogs for fishing bait
- Do scientific research to find the cause and solutions of amphibian diseases

Introduction of Exotic Species
- Prevent the introduction of predatory fish into breeding ponds
- Control the introduced Bullfrog population in British Columbia

Source: Conservation Priorities for the Amphibians and Reptiles of Canada, David and Carolyn Seburn for WWF Canada and CARCNET (2000)

You Can Help!

Populations of amphibians and reptiles are declining in Canada, and some have even disappeared completely. Habitat loss is happening far more rapidly than habitat re-growth. As their habitat disappears, so do entire populations of our reptiles and amphibians. Here are some ways you can help these innocent creatures survive.

Participate in Frogwatch

Frogwatch is part of a national volunteer monitoring program hosted by the Canadian Nature Federation and Environment Canada, to identify ecological changes that may be affecting our environment. Frogs are excellent indicator species because they spend part of their life in the water and part on land, and are affected by changes to either environment.

Frogwatch participants of all ages can help scientists monitor Canada's frogs. All you have to do is listen to frogs calling on a few evenings over the season, record your findings on the *Frogwatch* data form, and send the results to your area co-coordinator.

For more details on how you can help Canada's frogs, contact the Canadian Nature Federation at 1-800-267-4088, or check their website at http://www.cnf.ca/frog/.

Nominate an Important Amphibian and Reptile Area

Important Amphibian and Reptile Areas (IMPARAS) are areas that have special significance for the conservation of these animals. These areas are of immediate conservation importance because if they were lost, our natural heritage of amphibians and reptiles would be seriously endangered.

Conservationists need to identify critical habitat areas so that governments, developers and the public can know in advance which areas are important to the conservation of these animals. **The Canadian Amphibian and Reptile Conservation Network (CARCNET)** has created this program to do just that.

For more details on how you can participate, check the CARCNET website at http://www.carcnet.ca or e-mail apalone_trionyx@yahoo.com

North American Centre for Amphibian Malformations (NARCAM)

In the summer of 1995, school students on a field trip in Minnesota discovered large numbers of frogs with misshapen, extra or missing limbs. Since then, there has been a dramatic increase in reports of malformed amphibians in North America.

NARCAM has initiated a website designed for people to report sightings of amphibian malformations in North America. Regardless of whether you have seen malformed amphibians or have handled a number of wild amphibians without noticing anything wrong, they want to hear from you. Forms can be located on the website for both technical experts and non-biologists.

For more details, e-mail NARCAM at narcam@usgs.gov, or check their website at http://www.npwrc.usgs.gov/narcam/idguide/index.htm

Head for the hills!

All public libraries have a variety of amphibian and reptile identification guides. Grab a guide, gather up your family, friends or school class and head for the outdoors! Listen for frogs in the evening! Sit quietly in the outdoors and think about what kind of amphibians and reptiles might be quietly sharing the same space.

Visit your local zoo or reptile rescue centre and talk to the people who work with these animals. They will be more than happy to talk about their charges! Talk to your local naturalist club and maybe go on a guided walk to look for reptiles or amphibians.

Because the very best way we can help these animals is to learn about them. Their continued existence in our country depends on people knowing where they live and how many there are in any given area. You can be one of those people.

So go searching—but <u>remember to look and not touch!!</u>

Etcetera

Salamanders

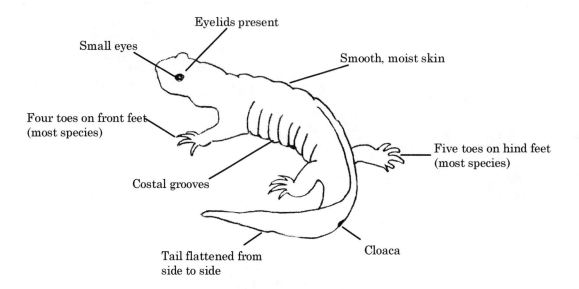

Eyelids present

Small eyes

Smooth, moist skin

Four toes on front feet
(most species)

Five toes on hind feet
(most species)

Costal grooves

Tail flattened from
side to side

Cloaca

Frogs & Toads

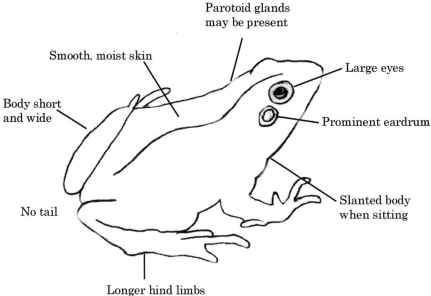

Parotoid glands
may be present

Smooth, moist skin

Large eyes

Body short
and wide

Prominent eardrum

No tail

Slanted body
when sitting

Longer hind limbs

Turtles

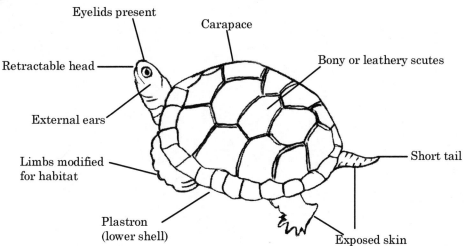

Eyelids present

Carapace

Bony or leathery scutes

Retractable head

External ears

Short tail

Limbs modified
for habitat

Plastron
(lower shell)

Exposed skin

Lizards

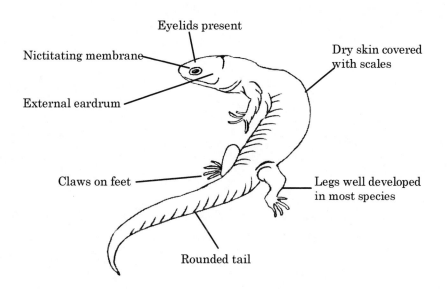

Eyelids present

Nictitating membrane

Dry skin covered
with scales

External eardrum

Claws on feet

Legs well developed
in most species

Rounded tail

Snakes

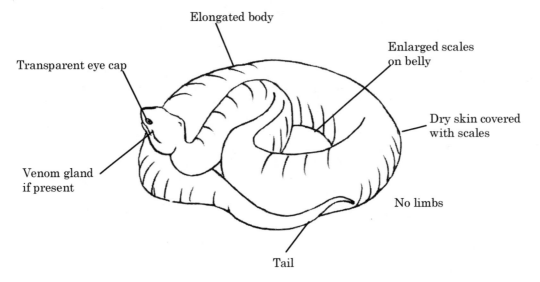

Elongated body

Enlarged scales on belly

Transparent eye cap

Dry skin covered with scales

Venom gland if present

No limbs

Tail

Teacher's Guide

Alberta's Reptiles: Lending a Helping Hand (or two or three) is a tool for Grade Seven teachers to help teach the science unit. It's an exciting guide full of information and activities that will get students thinking about their attitudes towards reptiles, and becoming familiar with the needs of reptiles. When you learn about reptile adaptations and the uniqueness of a *hibernaculum* (snake den), you will be awestruck at their distinctiveness. Reptiles are truly awesome!

The background information and activities are suitable for all provinces—just substitute your own snakes, lizards and turtles, as identified in *Canadian Skin and Scales*!

This expansive guide (103 pages) is available free from the Alberta Conservation Association. Visit their website at www.ab-conservation.com for more details, or contact them at the address below.

Alberta Conservation Association
7th Flr, O.S. Longman Building
6909—116 Street
Edmonton, AB T6H 4P2
Phone 1-877-969-9091

Canadian Internet Wildlife Links

◈ Amphibians of Canada http://collections.ic.gc.ca/amphibians
◈ Bird Studies Canada http://www.bsc-eoc.org/bscmain.html
◈ Birding in Canada http://www.web-nat.com/bic/
◈ Birds of North America http://www.birdsofna.org
◈ Canada's Aquatic Environments http://www.aquatic.uoguelph.ca/reptiles
◈ Canadian Amphibian and Reptile Conservation Network http://www.carcnet.ca
◈ Canadian Bird Conservation Program http://199.212.18.79/birds/mbirds.html
◈ Canadian Bird Trends Database http://www.cws-scf.ec.gc.ca/index_3.crm
◈ Canadian Museum of Nature http://www.nature.ca
◈ Canadian Nature Federation http://www.cnf.ca/
◈ Canadian Wildlife Federation http://www.cwf-fcf.org/
◈ Canadian Wildlife Service http://www.cws-scf.ec.gc.ca
◈ Committee on the Status of Endangered Wildlife In Canada (COSEWIC)
    http://www.cosewic.gc.ca
◈ Convention on International Trade in Endangered Species (CITES)
    http://www.cws-scf.ec.gc.ca/cites/intro_e.html
◈ Critter Crossings: Linking Habitats and Reducing Roadkill
    http://www.fhwa.dot.gov/environment/wildlifecrossings/main.htm
◈ Ducks Unlimited Canada http://www.ducks.ca
◈ Fatal Light Awareness Program http://www.flap.org/home2.html
◈ Important Bird Areas of Canada http://www.ibacanada.com
◈ North American Reporting Centre for Amphibian Malformations
    http://www.npwrc.usgs.gov/narcam/idguide/index.htm
◈ Peregrine Foundation http://www.peregrine-foundation.ca
◈ Space for Species http://www.spaceforspecies.ca
◈ Species At Risk Act http://www.speciesatrisk.gc.ca

Words To Know

Anal glands—an organ located near the tail of an animal that produces a chemical secretion

Aquatic—adapted to life in the water

Arboreal—adapted to life in the trees and branches

Bask—to hold the body in a position directly exposed to the sun

Camouflage—colours or patterns that help an animal hide by blending in with its surroundings

Cannibalistic—eating the flesh of one's own species

Carapace—the upper section of a turtle's shell

Carnivorous—an animal that feeds on other animals or animal matter

Clutch—eggs laid by a female during a single breeding event

Constriction—method used by snakes to kill prey, where they wrap their coils around the animal until it suffocates

Costal grooves—loose folds of skin indicating the position of the ribs in salamanders

Courtship—ritual behaviour between males and females that precedes mating

Culinary—referring to an item eaten by humans as food

Diurnal– active during the day

Embryo—young animal growing inside an egg or its mother

Fertilization—the combining of sperm and eggs to make a new organism

Flash colours—very bright colours on the underside of animals, designed to startle predators

Foraging—wandering about to search for food

Fracture points—the area in a lizard's tail where the muscles break cleanly apart

Fragile tail—a tail that the animal can break off at will

Freeze tolerant—species that undergo a physical process which keeps them from freezing solid during the winter

Gills—organs in an aquatic animal used to breathe oxygen from water

Gregarious—living in groups

Hibernate—to spend the winter in a dormant, or sleeping state

Hibernation—a long state of inactivity where all body functions slow down

Incubation—keeping eggs warm so that development is possible

Invertebrates—animals without backbones, such as insects

Iridescent—colours that shimmer in a rainbow effect

Larvae—the stage of an animal's life after it hatches from the egg but is not yet in the adult form

Melanistic—an over abundance of black pigment in the skin

Metabolic rate—the rate of energy expended by an animal

Metamorphosis—the changing of an animal from one stage of its life history to another, such as from larvae to adult

Migrate (tion)—making periodic journeys to and from breeding and wintering sites

Musk glands—an organ of the body that produces a foul smelling scent

Neotenic—animals who do not change into adult form, but remain and reproduce in the larval stage

Nocturnal—active at night

Orders—a method of classifying animal life into similar groups

Parotoid glands—a pair of glands on the shoulder, neck or behind the eye that produce a toxic substance

Pigment—a coloured substance in the skin or outer layer of an organism

Plastron– the lower part of a turtle's shell

Porous—allowing liquid to pass through gradually

Prehensile—able to grasp objects by wrapping around them

Scute—small, individual shields that cover the outside of turtle shells

Sperm—the sex cells from a male animal that unite with the egg produced by the female

Tadpoles—the larvae of a frog or toad

Temperate regions—areas of the Earth between the tropics and the polar regions

Terrestrial—adapted to life on the ground

Territory—an area occupied by individuals or breeding pairs which is defended against intruders

Toxic—a poisonous substance that kills or injures when swallowed or absorbed

Tubercles—small, knoblike projections

Under story—growth of shrubs, small bushes and thick grass underneath large trees

Venomous—a term for snakes and lizards that produce a poison in their bodies

Vertebrates—animals with a backbone

Vocal sac—a loose flap of skin that is extended during vocalizations to amplify the sound

Resources Used

Alderton, David - Turtles & Tortoises of the World, Facts on File Inc, 1988

Badger, David - Frogs, Voyager Press, 1995

Behler, King, J.L, Wayne F - Audubon Society Field Guide: North American Reptiles and Amphibians, Alfred A Knopf 1979

Carwardine, Mark - Guinness Book of Animal Records, Guinness Publishing, 1995

Clarke, Dr. Barry - Eyewitness Books: Amphibians, Stoddart Publishing Company Limited, 1993

Cochran, Doris M, Goin, C.J. - New Field Book of Reptiles & Amphibians, G.P. Putnam's Sons, 1970

Cook, Francis R - Introduction to Canadian Amphibians & Reptiles, National Museum of Natural Sciences, 1984

Discovery Books - Reptiles & Amphibians: An Explore Your World Handbook, Random House Inc, 2000

Ernst, C.H, Barbour R.W - Turtles of the World, Smithsonian Institution Press, 1989

Froom, Barbara - The Turtles of Canada, McClelland & Stewart Limited, 1976

Froom, Barbara - The Snakes of Canada, McClelland & Stewart Limited, 1972

Greene, Harry W - Snakes: The Evolution of Mystery in Nature, University of California Press, 1997

Halliday, Dr. Tim, Adler, Dr Craig - Firefly Encyclopaedia of Reptiles & Amphibians, Facts on File Inc, 2002

Long, K - Frogs Wildlife Handbook, Johnson Books, 1999

Mattison, Chris - Lizards of the World, Facts on File Inc, 1989

McCarthy, Colin - Eyewitness Books: Reptiles, Stoddart Publishing Co Lim, 1991

Tyning, Thomas F - Stokes Nature Guides: Amphibians & Reptiles, Little, Brown and Company, 1990

Internet Resources

Amphibia Web
http://dlp.cs.berkeley.edu/aw/

Amphibians of Canada
http://collections.ic.gc.ca/amphibians/

Canada's Aquatic Environments
http://www.aquatic.uoguelph.ca/reptiles

Canadian Amphibian & Reptile Conservation Network
http://www.carcnet.ca

Canadian Nature Federation Frogwatch
http://www.cnf.ca/frog/index.html

Canadian Museum of Nature
http://www.nature.ca/notebooks

The EMBL Reptile Database
http://www.reptiliaweb.org

North American Reporting Centre for Amphibian Malformations
http://www.npwrc.usgs.gov/narcam/idguide/index.htm

University of Michigan Museum of Zoology
http://animaldiversity.unmz.umich.edu

A Note From The Author

When I was growing up, I spent many, many happy hours on my stomach, often in mud, at the edge of our local frog pond. My friend and I would watch the tadpoles, water boatmen, skimmers and various other citizens of the water with keen fascination. Sometimes we would be lucky enough to catch a tadpole or frog and study them for a while before returning them to the water. After all these years, I can still feel them wriggling in my cupped palm!

Our frog pond hours were the most popular activity of my childhood, and began a lifelong interest in pond life and the smaller, forgotten creatures of our world. Sadly, our little pond is now the site of an apartment complex, a situation all too common in the world of amphibians and other wildlife today.

Many years later, as an education volunteer at our local zoo, I was lucky enough to have the task of teaching visitors that snakes are not slimy, 'yucky' or cold. I still have a long-dead watch because the strap has teeth holes in it made by baby boa constrictors. It is one of my most prized possessions!

By writing this book, I hope to give back to the amphibians and reptiles that have passed through and enriched my life. These amazing animals are worthy of our deepest respect, for without them we would all be knee deep in mice and mosquitoes! As with all wild creatures today, these animals need our help to survive. Perhaps when people read this book they will realize that these animals should not be thought of as bad or scary, but rather respected and appreciated for the helpful, fascinating creatures they are. *Pat Bumstead*

About the Illustrator

Norm Worsley was born in England in 1924, and has been drawn to the arts since he was nine years old. He attended Rochester Technical College of Art, specializing in Technical Drawing and General Arts. He entered the British Army and served with the Corps of Royal Engineers as instructor at a School of Military Engineers.

On leaving the services, Norm worked as a design engineer for a major construction company, and he and his family emigrated to Canada in 1976. After his retirement in 1988, Norm returned to his first love of drawing wildlife. Along with Edna, his wife of 58 years, he spends his time researching and drawing wildlife of the world. His work has been featured in several books: Canadian Feathers, Feline Facts, The 2x2 Guide to Zoo Animals, as well as numerous posters, brochures and newsletters. He donates all his work, preferring the sharing of knowledge to monetary gain.